# Japan

# Abduction & Deprivation of Freedom

# for the Purpose of Religious

# De-conversion

## Edited by Willy Fautre

1

**Contact address**

**Human Rights Without Frontiers International**

Avenue d'Auderghem 61/16,

1040 Brussels, Belgium

Tel/ Fax: +32-2-3456145

www.hrwf.org

Email: international.secretariat.brussels@hrwf.net

## Table of Contents

3

# EXECUTIVE SUMMARY

This report by *Human Rights Without Frontiers* (HRWF), an independent nongovernmental organization, documents **the abduction and confinement of Japanese citizens for the purpose of religious de-conversion, and the failure of Japanese police and judicial authorities to investigate and prosecute those responsible for such cases of domestic violence. The failure to provide the victims of such kidnappings with equal protection under the law, and the impunity of those responsible, constitute a serious violation of the Japanese people's constitutionally guaranteed rights and the international human rights standards to which Japan is legally bound.**

**Chapter I provides an overview of Japanese religions in order to place this problem in general perspective.** The Japanese have a tradition of multiple religious engagements, primarily with Shinto and Buddhism. These engagements have formed part of a strong web of social expectations and obligations, and individuals' family and household identities, rather than a matter of personal faith. Following World War II, individualism emerged more strongly, weakening the forces of group identity and belonging. Numerous organized religious sects and Christian denominations offered alternatives, and some became associated with deviance and violence. **There has been a widespread fear of sects, and calls for protection and the preservation of Japanese traditions at the expense of religious freedom, setting the stage for a conflict with Japan's laws and international human rights obligations, which protect individual human rights.**

5

**Chapter II** contains the results of *Human Rights Without Frontiers'* investigations of the abduction and confinement of Japanese citizens for the purpose of religions de-conversion. **Around 20 victims, who were mainly members of the Unification Church and the Jehovah's Witnesses, were interviewed in 2010 and 2011, as well as journalists, lawyers, and experts. HRWF also met with 10 members of the Japanese Diet to discuss the issue.**

**The illegal kidnappings were all organized by victims' families acting in cooperation with "exit counselors" who together conspired to violate the law.** Parents' concerns were intensified by media hype about the dangers of sects. Abductions were carefully planned and executed. Victims were held against their will in isolated conditions. The abductions show the power of families - the perpetrators -to control information on the fate of offspring who disappeared from their normal lives, and the unwillingness of authorities to investigate.

**In captivity, victims were subjected to coercive attempts to de-convert them, mainly by pastors and members of Protestant churches with assistance from former members of new religions. Long term effects include Post Traumatic Stress Disorder (PTSD) and other severe psychological problems.**

**In an extreme case, Unification Church member Toro Goto was violently abducted and held in isolation for 12 years, during which he was ill-treated including by starvation. After his release in 2008, prosecutors declined to indict his kidnappers on grounds of insufficient evidence.**

**Indeed, all known complaints against parents and exit counselors have been declared ineligible. Police have been**

**passive and have failed to investigate well-documented complaints.**

**Chapter III** summarizes how these crimes and the failure to investigate and prosecute leading to impunity and denial of equal protection under the law violate international law. Japan's failure to ensure equal protection under the law by protecting citizens from de-conversion kidnappings is unequivocally at variance with Japan's treaty obligations as a signatory to the International Covenant on Civil and Political Rights (ICCPR) and rulings by the UN Human Rights Committee. Relevant US and European case law is also summarized.

**Chapter IV** contains recommendations for Japanese authorities, Japanese and international civil society, Japan's partners in the international community, and international institutions. The crimes documented in this Report must be brought to the international level, and international institutions and civil society should assist Japanese authorities to bring them to an end.

# INTRODUCTION

**By Dr Aaron Rhodes, Hamburg (Germany)[1]**

This report documents the abduction and confinement of Japanese citizens for the purpose of religious de-conversion, and the failure of Japanese police and judicial authorities to investigate and prosecute those responsible. The failure to provide the victims of such kidnappings with equal protection under the law, and the impunity of those responsible, constitute a serious violation of the Japanese people's constitutionally guaranteed rights and the international human rights standards to which Japan is legally bound.

Japanese politicians and civil society and the international human rights community have ignored this long-standing problem, which has had tragic consequences for perhaps thousands of people. This Report is meant to provide objective, empirical documentation, cultural and legal background and analysis, and recommendations in the hope that

---

[1] Aaron Rhodes is an international human rights advocate, university lecturer and essayist. Between 1993 and 2007, he was Executive Director of the International Helsinki Federation for Human Rights (Vienna). In 2008 he and several colleagues established the International Campaign for Human Rights in Iran. He also held positions at Boston University and the Institute for Human Sciences in Vienna. He was educated at Reed College and at The University of Chicago, where he was awarded a PhD in the Committee on Social Thought.

Japanese and international authorities, and civil society, will take long-overdue steps to end it.

Most observers of international human rights issues would likely be surprised to learn of a major human rights problem in Japan, one of the most law-abiding, civilized and literate societies in the world. Japan is not a focus of intense scrutiny by the international human rights community, which has its hands full addressing issues where, unlike in Japan, governments have no respect for the rule of law and international standards.

At the same time, members of minority religions often face discrimination and abuse in the most advanced societies, discrimination that has often received too little attention and has been allowed to persist because of prejudices that blind even enlightened activists to these problems. Many members of the public show little concern for the problems of members of religious organizations whose beliefs and practices they disapprove of, and relativise their problems with reference to the alleged breaches of ethics and law they attribute to such groups.

It should go without saying that religious organizations are obliged to operate within the law in any society. If they break laws, they should be charged and punished. But they and their members cannot be allowed to be denied freedom and protection because of unsubstantiated charges and prejudices. In fact, many new religions and minority religions, including those in Japan, suffer violations of their members' human rights because they pose a threat to other denominations that seek to preserve their "market share" sometimes with the assistance of the authorities. The moral integrity and faithfulness to human rights and democratic principles of any society is always tested by how it tolerates religious minorities.

The Japanese authorities and civil society are also being tested because the abductions are a form of domestic violence; they are typically organized by victims' own families, and are thus the most difficult kind of crime to address out of respect for privacy and the efforts of families to protect their respect and honor. But if Japanese authorities are serious about respecting individual human rights as defined by international law, they cannot dredge up cultural relativism arguments to justify violations of human rights on the basis of a particular Japanese tradition of family sovereignty.

I became acutely aware of kidnappings and sometimes violent attempts to force Japanese citizens to renounce their faith during a visit to Tokyo in 2010, during which I met victims, got an overview of the problem, and, along with Dr. Willem Frederik van Eekelen, former Netherlands Former Minister of Defence and Deputy Foreign Minister, conferred with ten members of the Japanese Diet to gain a perspective on how the government views the issue. For decades these cases have been exposed in public, but the absence of moral outrage, especially in a society known for its capacity for self-criticism, shame, and mobilization around moral causes, was clear. Politicians were generally unwilling to engage publicly, and some who acknowledged the problem said the police were not fully accountable under the system; journalists were generally uninterested; and no local human rights organizations seem to have taken up the issue. Abductees and their families were traumatized by what had happened to them and deeply frustrated by the inaction of the authorities and the indifference to their plight.

The only serious documentation of the cases has been done by religious organizations, primarily the Unification Church, whose members have been the main victims of the kidnappings but victims are never considered fully reliable and authoritative sources of evidence about the crimes they have suffered.

In seeking an institutional partner to analyze this problem and thus fill a serious gap in the human rights literature, *Human Rights Without Frontiers* was the obvious choice, as it has more expertise and experience on issues of religious freedom than any other independent human rights organization, as well as an unblemished reputation for objective, scientific work.

One of the politicians we met in 2010 said Japan needed a "black ship" to help it deal with this issue, referring to the push toward international integration and modernity provided by the arrival of Admiral Perry in 1853. We sensed a feeling of resignation about how Japan's unique culture had left a residue of intractable attitudes that, despite a veneer of technocratic rationality, left Japan's institutions unable to change and the society isolated from the rest of the world. But the ultimate conclusion to be drawn from the kidnappings of members of minority religions should be different. Many other societies have faced similar problems, and many—perhaps most—still have problems to fully reconcile their international obligations to protect individual human rights with traditions and with powerful, even compulsive urges to conform to expectations rooted in family or clan structures.

Japan is, in fact, not alone in this regard, and Japan can refer to human rights standards that bring the international community together, and provide guidance and solidarity. Japanese authorities can find much constructive assistance from the

12

international human rights community in rectifying the problem. In presenting this report, we hope to raise awareness and to encourage a broad dialogue about the kidnappings. We hope to encourage and support a credible and effective institutional response at the national and international level. We are optimistic that the problem of the kidnappings can and will end.

# OVERVIEW: JAPANESE RELIGIONS IN GENERAL PERSPECTIVE

**By Prof. Ian Reader, University of Manchester (UK)[2]**

While a number of religious traditions have been active in Japan over the centuries, the various traditions share some common ground, with interaction between them being perhaps more prevalent than conflict or strife. Religious belonging, too, has often been not so much a 'this or that' matter of exclusive choice, as is common in many cultures and contexts, but has been more a matter of engagement with multiple traditions, with participation in a variety of practices, rituals and events at different religious institutions depending on context and circumstances, being the norm. The two most prevalent traditions in this context have been Shinto and Buddhism, and the two have been embedded together in the social and cultural history and customs of Japan ever since Buddhism first came to Japan in the 6th century CE. Shinto and Buddhism have long

---

[2] Ian Reader has researched and taught about religion in Japan for over a quarter of a century. He has held academic positions in the fields of Religious Studies and in Japanese Studies at institutions in Japan, Hawaii, Scotland, Denmark and England. From 1999-2006 he was Professor of Religious Studies at Lancaster University. Since 2007 he has been Professor of Japanese Studies at the University of Manchester, but will return in 2012 to Lancaster as Professor of Religious Studies. His publications include several books and articles about the dynamics of religion in modern Japan, and one of the main areas of his recent research has been on the Japanese religious movement, Aum Shinrikyo, that carried out the 1995 attack on the Tokyo subway, and on how this has affected public perceptions of religion in Japan.

played major parts in the socio-cultural system through which the majority of Japanese people have engaged with religious traditions, and they are associated with a variety of customary and complementary practices and concepts related to social belonging and to life-cycles, ranging from ceremonies relating to the birth of babies to rituals at death.

Besides Shinto and Buddhism, a number of other religious traditions have influenced the Japanese milieu or developed a presence there, from Confucianism, which has never been an independent religious tradition in Japan but which has influenced the ways Buddhism developed in East Asia, to the various new religions that have developed in Japan in the modern era, since the early nineteenth century. The new religions (a generic term used to refer to the large numbers of movements that have developed in Japan, mostly drawing extensively on Shinto, Buddhist and folk traditions, and led by charismatic Japanese leaders) initially developed around individual conversion rather than social belonging, and from the early nineteenth to the late twentieth century, several waves of new religions have appeared. As new religions have grown older and developed second-generation (and beyond) followers they have relied increasingly not on conversion but on social belonging to sustain their memberships, and this in turn has produced a tendency towards conservatism and adherence to socially normative patterns.

Overall, new religions have tended to fit into the broader Japanese religious spectrum and have not challenged the socio-cultural standing of Shinto and Buddhism or participation in customary rites associated with Shinto and Buddhism.

There have, however, been some notable exceptions among the new religions to this pattern. of not challenging the status quo in socio-cultural terms, leading to some major problems and conflicts to be mentioned later. In addition, Christianity has had a presence- initially via foreign missionaries- since Japan opened up its borders to outside forces from the mid-nineteenth century, although it has never acquired any significant following in Japan, with support levels remaining around one per cent at most, and in recent times, too, a small number of other religious movements have entered Japan from abroad- notably the Jehovah's Witnesses, the Church of Jesus Christ of Latter-day Saints (Mormons) and the Unification Church- and engaged in proselytization activities there.

**Social contexts, individual rights and areas of contention**

In general, social context has been a dominant element in terms of religious association and adherence, with the general Japanese emphasis on the household (Japanese: - a term that traditionally referred to the extended family structure, and in Japan included not just living members but also the deceased who were venerated as ancestors, and the generations yet to come and for whom the *ie* was to be preserved and continued) as the primary unit of social belonging and identity being central here.

People were until modern times regarded primarily as members of a social unit- their *ie* as well as their local community- and it was via their belonging to these units that their religious affiliations and obligations were manifested. As such, participation in various practices such as Buddhist rituals for the household dead and attendance at community events and festivals at the local Shinto shrine were incumbent on people

17

because they were expected, as members of the social unit, to do such things. This did not mean that people were not able to hold individual beliefs or engage in specialised practices. Indeed, there has long been a religious free market in such contexts, with people choosing, if they so wished, to supplement their traditional obligations (to household and community rituals) with individual worship of specific deities, Buddhist practices such as meditation or chanting sutras, going on pilgrimages to prominent shrines and temples, and so on. They have tended to do so, however, in conjunction with engaging in the aforementioned socially and customarily agreed practices that confirm a sense of social belonging and harmony, and while people have always been able to engage in individual religious faith and practices, there has long been a widespread recognition that this should not come at the expense of conforming to practices associated with social belonging and obligation.

In the post-war era, however, a variety of forces, from urbanisation to changing social structures, have stimulated the rise of individualism and weakened traditional notions of group identity and belonging. The *ie* itself has undergone changes, with an increasing number of households being nuclear, and increasing numbers simply not marrying or continuing the *ie* tradition, and this too has eroded the sense of social and cultural obligation that has traditionally emphasised participation. Moreover, with the promulgation of the 1946 Constitution, which guarantees the freedom of religious worship and association, the prime emphasis in religious terms, legally, is now on the rights of the individual who, once s/he has attained majority (20) age, is free to join and participate (or not) in religious activities of his/her own volition. In theory the individual, once having attained legal majority age, is protected in this by law, and is in theory not subject to social or family expectations or commands.

This emphasis on individual autonomy, however, has caused some tensions with expectations still widely held about the importance of adhering to commonly assumed social norms related to religion and to participation in customary (especially household-related) activities and rituals. In particular, problems have arisen in recent times when the exercise of individual religious freedom and choice involves a rejection of such cultural customs and norms embedded in Japanese social and familial structures. Such problems have been exacerbated by the fact that religion as an organised entity has acquired a highly negative image in Japan since the 1995 attack on the Tokyo subway by the new religious group Aum Shinrikyo. Aum specifically rejected customary social norms and encouraged devotees to sever ties with their families, and its participation in crimes such as the subway attack appeared, to many Japanese, to suggest that any religious group that went against social norms could be dangerous, especially if, as with Aum, it combined rejection of the family and social customs, with an emphasis on complete devotion to the religion concerned and to its leadership structures. Such worries have also spurred widespread demands in Japan – upheld repeatedly in surveys of public opinion– that steps should be taken to protect society from any group that goes against conventional Japanese social mores and to extricate people from such groups wherever possible.

Shinto and Buddhism are, as has been noted, historically the main religious traditions of Japan. The word 'Shinto' means the 'way of the gods' and the tradition associated with it developed from amorphous folk customs, practices and beliefs that coalesced into a formal, named tradition after the arrival of Buddhism in Japan. Shinto is centred on Japan and its people. Central to Shinto is the notion of kami – 'gods' or spiritual forces of varying influences, from powerful kami venerated throughout Japan to localised figures particular to one location or area. Shinto myths speak of Japan as a country of myriad kami that give life to the country and support its people in their endeavours.

Shinto is ethnically based in that it is centred on Japan and its people, and it is grounded in myths and legends that suggest that it was via the life-giving acts of the kami that the land and people of Japan first emerged. The kami also are portrayed in myths as ancestors of the Japanese Imperial family, and Shinto has thus had a nationalist orientation in which Emperor, nation and people are linked together.

For most people, however, Shinto is primarily a local customary affair. Kami serve as protectors of local communities and local shrines operate as a focus for community rituals. People visit the shrines to seek the help of kami at important times in life – students and schoolchildren pray for support prior to examinations; lovers visit shrines associated with love and marriage to pray for a partner; parents take new-born babies to the shrine for a blessing that places them under the protection of the kami; and the community gathers to celebrate popular national festivals. At New Year, for example, most Japanese make the first shrine visit of the year to seek the protection of the kami for the coming year – a practice in which approximately two-thirds of the nation engages in during the first three days of each year, usually doing so with family or friends and often dressed in traditional Japanese kimono, making for an event rich in social enjoyment, national celebration and custom.

Buddhism reached Japan 1000 years after its origination in India. It came via China and Korea and absorbed many influences there- notably from Confucianism, whose focus on performing rituals for the dead and venerating them as ancestors, and on the extended family as a unit both of social and religious practice deeply influenced Buddhism. In Japan, Buddhism has produced several important philosophical traditions, moral teachings and ways of practice associated with salvation and spiritual advancement, along with numerous other practices and figures of worship designed to ameliorate life in this world. However, its deepest significance for most Japanese has been in providing explanations of what happens at death and in offering rituals and practices that enable the living to care for the dead and help them in the after-life. Such practices and concepts are particularly centred on the family and household, with a common set of customs and beliefs that the dead should be cared for after death by their kin, and that when done properly the dead can attain peace and become benevolent ancestors guarding the living and their future kin.

During the Tokugawa (1600-1867) era the *danka* system commanded all Japanese households to be affiliated with and have death-related rituals performed at local Buddhist temples, ; the term *danka* means a household belonging to and supporting a Buddhist temple. Traditionally there was no sense of individual choice; people were associated with Buddhism because of their familial belonging, and while this system was legally abolished in the nineteenth century, its imprint has remained strong. It is widely believed that at death the spirit retains a link to this world, and that through appropriate

21

Buddhist rituals the deceased can become a benevolent ancestor caring for its living kin and for the future generations of the household. Members of households have thus had an obligation to perform the appropriate services for the deceased to facilitate this- and to provide peace in death for their deceased kin. To a great degree, this has meant that the older generations rely on or hope that their offspring will care for them when they die- as they had done for their parents.

Support structures for Buddhism have eroded in modern times, especially as the influence of the *ie* has waned because of changing social structures, and as beliefs in the ancestors and an afterlife have declined in what is an increasingly modern society. However, there remains a strong undercurrent of feeling, especially in more traditional households, that individuals continue to have an obligation in this area and that, even if they have different views, they should subordinate them for the benefit of the wider social unit of the household and thereby give comfort to their parents and grandparents. Thus, those who may join a new religion or reject Buddhism are often expected to continue upholding familial practices related to the ancestors, and to a great extent, the wider public view supports families that expect their members to follow such conventions.

Much engagement in religious contexts related to Shinto and Buddhism has thus been mainly of social custom and practice than of belief or personal commitment. Thus, most Japanese answer in surveys that they are 'not religious' –a stance that indicates that they do not have specific, committed sets of belief in a particular religion – yet will also say that they take part in Buddhist rituals associated with the dead, as well as traditional Shinto practices such as attending local shrine festivals and making a New Year shrine visit. Such practices are complementary in that people may readily attend and engage in both Shinto and Buddhist practices and events without seeing any contradiction or considering that this indicates any specific religious affiliation or belief. Indeed, personal belief (or lack thereof) is not seen as a barrier to such participation and to a certain degree there remains an element of bemusement among many Japanese that people might refuse to do such things because of their personal religious orientations.

## New religions, Christianity and the emergence of alternative religions

From the early nineteenth century, a number of new religious movements developed in Japan, usually centred around revelations and spiritual insights claimed by charismatic individuals. These 'new religions', as they came to be known, often drew extensively on the existing religious environment – for example, using concepts derived from Buddhism or associations with particular Shinto kami – but they also offered ordinary people opportunities to acquire spiritual techniques that helped them deal with personal problems and to find new means of individual salvation. Such movements have been eclectic and highly diverse in nature, yet they share enough common ground and characteristics to be labelled under the broad general category of 'new religions' (the term 'new' – *shin* in Japanese– standing in contrast to the 'established'– *kisei*– traditions of Shinto and Buddhism). Their initial attraction was to individuals, many of whom were drawn by the charisma of the founders of such movements and their claims of spiritual healing and new means of acquiring personal success and salvation. While such conversions could cause problems if such converts forsook their traditional social obligations, it has been more common for new religions to avoid any confrontation with normative socio-cultural practices, and many have continued to encourage their members to participate in Buddhist funerals and Shinto rituals. To that degree, many new religions have managed to avoid controversy by fitting into the broader pattern of social norms.

Nonetheless, new religions in general have a negative reputation and have faced much social resistance and opprobrium because they do provide alternatives to the religious and social establishments in Japan, and because some of their success has come at the expense of the older traditions. New religions have often been denounced by the media and by the older traditions as being 'false religions' because they threaten the wellbeing of the established traditions and appear capable of undermining the general social cohesion. The founders (many of whom claimed they had been chosen by powerful deities to radically change the world and create a new spiritual civilisation) have often been portrayed as extreme and irrational. In addition, the success of some of these movements has at times been so striking that it has caused the Japanese establishment serious concerns, especially in the late nineteenth and early twentieth century. New movements such as Omoto, led by the charismatic Deguchi Onisaburo, acquired millions of followers while espousing strong critiques of Japanese society, and demanding social and spiritual transformation in Japan. Prior to 1945, several new religions were suppressed for appearing to challenge the state, and it was not until after the 1946 constitution, with its guarantees of freedom of worship, that new religions were free from the threat of state interference and control.

Although many new religions have conformed to social patterns and advised followers to uphold traditional obligations, a small number have taken a different stance, and these have not only proved to be highly controversial, but have come to be seen (somewhat incorrectly) as representative of new religions in general. One such example has been Soka Gakkai, a lay Buddhist movement of the Nichiren Buddhist tradition. It grew rapidly in the post-war era, becoming the largest single religious movement in Japan and initially proclaiming, in its period of massive expansion, the goal of converting all Japanese and turning Japan into a state governed by its vision of Buddhist law. This vision of control– spurred also by aggressive proselytization campaigns that led to numerous complaints against the Gakkai and coupled with the Gakkai's sense of exclusivity that led members to withdraw from social and community practices– has caused widespread fear and anathema in Japan. The Gakkai has also developed a political profile through establishing a political party (Komeito) that has acquired a significant number of Diet members and has been a junior partner in recent coalition governments. While this political association has been of value to the movement, it has also helped fuel suspicions among the general public about Soka Gakkai's ambitions, and there remains a groundswell of hostility in Japan to the movement.

Another area of religious engagement of relevance- and one that has had the capacity for social discord- has been the arrival of Christianity in Japan. It came first in the sixteenth century, but after a brief period in which it gained a following among some feudal fiefdoms, it was banned due to fears (based in a growing Japanese awareness of its role in the colonial subjugation of other lands) that it threatened the integrity and independence of Japan. Allowed to re-enter when Japan opened its doors to Western forces in the mid-nineteenth century, Catholic and various Protestant denominations have since made efforts to develop a following in Japan. They have had some influences through education (setting up schools, for example, and gaining some support among the Japanese elite) and social welfare activities, but overall Christianity has been relatively unsuccessful in Japan, and it remains marginal numerically. Key reasons for its relative failure are that it has gone against the traditional cultural grain of religions in Japan, both because of its rejection of the concept of ancestors, which has conflicted with the importance traditionally placed on them in Japan, and its emphasis on a single monolithic all-powerful deity, which does not fit well with the Japanese notion of multiple figures of worship. Its demands (whether Catholic or Protestant) for singular belonging do not fit well with the notion of multiple adherence that holds sway in Japan.

**Problems and conflicts: individual belief and the rejection of customary practices**

The cases of Christianity and Soka Gakkai indicate that a sense of unease can emerge when religions appear to go against the cultural consensus mentioned above. In recent times, such issues have become significant in the public sphere in Japan because new religious groups– including those from outside Japan– have emerged that have been particularly ardent in their emphasis on exclusivity, leading them to confront or reject traditional family- and community- based notions and customs. When such groups then either become engaged in illegal activities or are perceived to be a source of social unease and danger, such perceptions have been exacerbated further, and they have had repercussions on other religions as a result. The most striking example has been Aum Shinrikyo. This movement grew in the 1980s and attracted a small number of highly dedicated followers, most of whom were young and highly educated yet deeply alienated from modern materialistic society. Aum developed a communal monastic-style system focused on absolute devotion to its spiritual leader (Asahara Shoko) and encouraged devotees to renounce their families and family names, donate all their possessions to Aum, take up monastic orders and a new 'holy name' in Aum. Such demands brought Aum into conflict with families whose offspring left home, and a number of legal battles raged as families tried to gain access to offspring who had become Aum converts. Those over the legal age of majority were fully entitled to do so under the law, but public opinion clearly sided with the parents. When Aum became enmeshed in successive conflicts- not just with parents of devotees but with local communities where it had built its communes, and then with journalists and lawyers involved in campaigns against Aum- the tensions evident between it and society at large became ever-greater. This fed into Aum's belief that it had to fight against mainstream society in order to destroy the current material civilisation and bring about world spiritual transformation – and was a factor in Aum's turn to violence that culminated in public attacks such as the 1995 Tokyo subway attack. This was a cathartic and transformative event in Japan. Not only had a religious movement committed mass murder, but evidence emerged that it had been able to shield behind the laws protecting religion from state interference and had benefitted from tax breaks given to religious groups, thereby enabling it to finance its secret chemical weapons making activities. The affair has given rise to extensive debates in Japan about what the limits of religious freedom might be, about the levels of scrutiny public security agencies ought to be allowed over religious groups, and about the extent to which religions should be allowed to acquire funds and to proselytise. Many surveys now show that there is a widespread public opposition to religious groups being able to proselytise in public spaces and a widespread public wish for closer state scrutiny of religious groups.

The Aum affair has deeply coloured the debates about how to deal with other religious groups that appear to go against social norms and have exclusivist views. Particularly after Aum's crimes, many in Japan claimed that members of the group must have been in some way 'brainwashed' to make them so radically confrontational with society and to have joined such a movement. The notion of 'brainwashing' or 'mind control' was particularly resonant in Japan because Aum devotees had rejected their biological families, entered Aum communes, and expressed undying devotion to their leader, Asahara – a devotion so extreme that some were prepared to kill on his behalf. While claims of 'brainwashing' or 'mind control' may be ungrounded in empirical terms (studies show that Aum members joined voluntarily and were willing participants rather than 'mind controlled' cyphers in their activities) the imprint of the affair continues to reverberate especially in two ways. First is that joining any religious group (especially one that rejects familial and social customs, and that demands total loyalty to a new creed) has come to be seen as especially "dangerous". While this view may have existed prior to Aum, it has become far more acute since. Second is that anyone who has joined such a group 'must' have been manipulated into doing so. Such views– based not in evidence but public assumption– remain potent and  have helped spur the growth of a militant 'anti-cult' movement in Japan and foster notions that people who join 'cults' (a term now widely applied in Japan to any group seen to be deviating from social norms and standing apart from the religious establishment) need to be 'rescued' from them.

The issue has become expressly contentious when movements explicitly repudiate social norms (as with the Unification Church's stance on the biological family or the Jehovah's Witnesses' refusal of blood transfusions), and withdrawal from household memorial practices concerning care for the dead. For parents in such circumstances, an offspring who ceases to participate in such practices may be seen as a danger to their (the parents') future solace if the offspring no longer is willing to perform the customary practices. This conflict between individual rights and concepts of individual religious freedom of choice, and social conventions centred on the community, household, family (and on inherent traditional notions that offspring, even if of legal majority age, should remain liable to parental influence) thus is a key area of discussion in contemporary Japanese religious contexts.

**Concluding remarks**

The multiplicity of religious traditions in Japan has by and large operated within a framework in which they interact and share much common ground. It is culturally and socially expected that people should engage in various practices and customs related to religion even if they do not consider themselves as believers. In such contexts, belonging is based not in individual belief so much as group and unity, and here one finds some tensions with the legal position of individual freedom. Overall, issues of difference have been managed relatively well, as with, for example, the ways in which most new religions are able to negotiate between individual adherence to such religions, and compliance with the social obligations incurred as members of households and communities. When movements break away from such socially held conventions, problems arise, among parents fearful that they will not be cared for or memorialised by their offspring after death, and among the wider public worried about 'deviant' and 'dangerous' religions – a notion that has significantly gained ground since 1995 and Aum. The public perception that those who join such 'deviant' groups (i.e. those that repudiate socially held norms) 'must' have been manipulated to do so, also contributes to conflicts and tensions between notions of individual rights that are legally guaranteed in Japan, and publicly and socially held conventions. These issues are central to the public treatment of people who have joined religious movements that go against Japanese social conventions, and to the ways such movements are perceived in Japan.

# REPORT OF FACT-FINDING MISSIONS

*Based on interviews conducted for Human Rights Without Frontiers in Tokyo, Seoul and Barcelona by Dr Aaron Rhodes (July 2010), Victoria Pirker (July 2011), Prof. Willy Fautré (August-September 2011) and Hans Noot (November 2011)*

**By Willy Fautré, Director of Human Rights Without Frontiers**[3]

In 2011, at least five adult converts to the Unification Church[4] were abducted by their parents for the purpose of religious de-conversion. In 2010 and 2009 there were nine and three known cases, respectively.

All but one of the converts were in their 30s and late 20s. Like most Japanese, their parents considered themselves non-religious but partook in some social Buddhist and Shinto

---

[3] Author of numerous articles on freedom of religion or belief such as:

**Religious intolerance in Belgium: The Role of Certain State and Non-state Actors** in Religion-Staat-Gesellschaft, Zeitschrift for Glaubensformen und Weltanschauungen/ Journal for the Study of Beliefs and Worldviews, 12. Jahrgang 2011, Heft 1, Technische Universität Dresden, pp 209-225.
**The Sect Issue in France and in Belgium**, pp 323-328, in Law and Religion/National, International and Comparative Perspectives by W. Cole Durham and Brett G. Scharffs (Wolters Kluwer), Aspen Publishers, 618 p. (2010).
**Religious Freedom Advocacy Opportunities at the European Parliament**, pp 391-400, in Religion - Staat - Gesellschaft, Journal for the Study of Beliefs and Worldviews, 10th Year, Issue 2.
[4] The Unification Church (UC), founded by the South Korean Reverend Moon, started its activities in Japan in 1959 and was incorporated on 16 July 1964.

practices[5]. Most of the converts were young women[6]. They mostly belonged to the middle class and had a university education background. A few had been abducted for the second time. Some could escape and kept their faith; some could leave after their family's unsuccessful attempts to de-convert them; some recanted their faith. In a few cases, the help of hostile former Unification Church members or anti-cult actors, including Protestant pastors, was requested by the parents.

The source of this information is a prolific independent Japanese journalist known for his articles, research papers and a book criticizing certain activities of new religious movements and cults: Kazuhiro Yonemoto[7]. However, despite his concerns about cults, in the last decade he discovered more cases of abduction perpetrated for the purpose of de-conversion, and had the intellectual honesty and concern for civil liberties and the

---

[5] Japanese usually practice the Shinto ritual at New Year, the Christian or Shinto rite for marriages and the Buddhist rite for funeral.

[6] Globally, there are more young women than young men in Japan's Unification Church. Hence probably the higher number of cases involving young women. Moreover, in the Japanese culture, many parents of the older generation still consider that their children, though adults, remain under their authority and owe them obedience during their whole life (Confucian influence). Hence probably the higher number of cases involving young women.

[7] He mentioned the list of cases registered in 2009-2011 in a letter dated 26 July 2011 and addressed to Alexander McLaren, Public Diplomacy Officer, Office of International Religious Freedom, U.S. Department of State in Washington.

Kazuhiro Yonemoto is known for having published articles criticizing new religious movements and cults in Japan, such as 'Happy Science Group', 'Life Space', 'Yamagishi Kai', 'Shinran Kai', 'Kensei Kai', 'Houno Hana', 'Jehovah's Witnesses', 'Unification Church', 'Aum Shinrikyo' and 'Powerful Mate.' He also published several anti-cult books: 'Founder Arrested' (Takarajima), 'Inspiration to Ryuhou Okawa' (Takarajima) criticizing the founder of 'Happy Science Group', 'Paradise of Brainwashing – Tragedies in Yamagishi Kai' (Yosensha) and others.

law to publicize them. Moreover, the journalist interviewed two recent victims of abduction who managed to escape in 2010 - Miyuki Hara and Keiichi Murata, both from Tokyo – and published their testimonies on his blog (http://yonemoto.blog63.fc2.com)[8].

Yonemoto's investigation[9] contradicts the 2010 and 2011 Religious Freedom Reports of the US State Department which say, among other things, that the reports of the Unification Church concerning the abduction of several of their members these last two years "could not be independently confirmed."

Also noteworthy is the case filed before a civil court[10] by Toru Goto against family members and their exit counseling accomplices after his 12-year deprivation of freedom[11]. It must also be stressed that a number of exit counselors have publicly encouraged parents to abduct and deprive their children of their

---

[8] In 2002, Kazuhiro Yonemoto interviewed three women – Asako Shukuya, Misako Takasu and Hiromi Nakajima – who had left the Unification Church after being abducted, deprived of their freedom and submitted to unsolicited exit counseling. In 2004, he published an article based on these interviews and entitled "Untold saga and terrors of religious confinement" in the monthly magazine GEKKAN GENDAI in 2004 (the publisher, Kodansha, is known to be very critical to the Unification Church). The title of the blog means 'Flick Away'.

[9] Yonemoto has been monitoring this issue since 1999 as a researcher totally independent from the UC. His first article in 1999 was entitled 'Documentary: Drop Out'. Then, he wrote comprehensive and critical pieces over the forced de-conversion issue in magazine articles in 2004 and in the book 'Our Disturbing Neighbors' in 2008.

[10] Toru Goto filed a complaint against family members and their exit counselors before a civil court on 31 January 2011 after his request for criminal proceedings had been turned down by the Prosecutor's Office.

[11] The deprivation of freedom periods usually range from a few days or weeks to several months and sometimes more than a year.

freedom until they recant their new faith, in itself a possible violation of the law.

In his book "Unification Church: Rescue and Rehabilitation" published by *Inochinokotobasha* (Word of Life) in September 1994, Tamiya Taguchi[12], a former member of the movement who converted to Protestantism, makes detailed recommendations about each phase of the 'rescue operation': the recruitment of relatives to perform the abduction, the search for an apartment and its adaptation to confinement conditions, the rental contract, the household utensils to be chosen or avoided, the meals, the possible visit of the police, and so on.

In the minutes of a "Lost Youth Compensation"[13] lawsuit, Mamoru Takazawa (pastor of an "independent" Protestant Church) recognizes his involvement in abduction, deprivation of freedom for the purpose of de-conversion.

Last but not least, three judgments by civil courts in 2002 and 2004 confirmed the practice of abduction and deprivation of freedom for the purpose of religious de-conversion, declared illegal the unsolicited exit counseling and condemned its perpetrators.

---

[12] Tamiya Taguchi was the former director of a UC training center. He died in 2002.

[13] Many members who left the UC were advised by anti-cult lawyers to file complaints for alleged damages suffered as a result of losing several years of their youth in the UC and to ask for financial compensation. The so-called "Lost Youth Compensation Cases" began in Sapporo City, Hokkaido, claiming that the witnessing activities conducted by the Unification Church members were illegal. Plaintiffs organized by anti-cult actors sought compensation for damages suffered as a result of losing several years of their youths while in the Church. The trial at Sapporo District Court lasted for 14 years from 1987 to 2001.

In the final decision of the case by Hiroko Tomizawa against her parents and the exit counselor Mamoru Takazawa, the Hiroshima Higher Court (Matsue branch) stated on 22 February 2002 that the parents had abducted their 31-year old daughter and deprived her of her freedom from 7 June 1997 to 30 August 1998, which was an illegal act, and "the appellant Takazawa provided assistance in the abduction and the confinement." Concerning the pastor, the judgment said: "The appellant, Takazawa, performed the act of persuasion while knowing that the respondent had been abducted and confined, which is illegal. He took advantage of such a situation. This is beyond the scope of a normal religious activity. The persuasion act performed by the appellant Takazawa was illegal. As an assistant, the appellant Takazawa shares the collective responsibility together with the parents" and the Higher Court ruled that "they must jointly pay 150,000 yen (1500 €)."

In the final decision of the case brought by Kozue Terada[14] against her parents and two exit counselors, Mamoru Takazawa and Atsuyoshi Ojima (lay assistant at a Lutheran Church), the Osaka High Court (9th Civil Section) ruled on 22 July 2004 that Kozue Terada's parents and Takazawa had jointly perpetrated an illegal act by imposing persuasion sessions against her will in a situation where she was under physical restraint, and condemned them to jointly pay 200,000 yen (2000 €) for depriving Kozue Terada of her freedom of movement (Joint tort). Ojima was declared innocent on the grounds that his

---

[14] Kozue Terada (Japanese) who was married to a South Korean citizen was living in her husband's country. She made a visit to her family and on that occasion was abducted and deprived of her freedom of movement by her parents. She was submitted to exit counseling against her will.

persuasion activity had been limited to a conversation, which was not illegal.

In the final decision of the case involving a female Jehovah's Witness abducted by her husband[15] with a pastor acting as an exit counselor, the 10th Civil Division of Osaka High Court composed of three judges ruled in 2002 that the pastor had been an accomplice in the confinement of the plaintiff as he had provided a building remodeled so as to prevent any escape, had collaborated in an act infringing upon her physical and psychological freedom, which was unlawful, and had taken concrete steps to do so[16]. The court dismissed the qualification of "pastoral activity" for the action of the religious minister and condemned him to the payment of 300,000 yen (3000 €) as compensation for the plaintiff and 100,000 yen as reimbursement for her attorney's fees.[17] It appears that this case had a deterrent effect, insofar as no other Jehovah's Witness has been abducted since then.

---

[15] She did not lodge a criminal complaint against the perpetrator because out of remorse he had released her after 17 days of confinement. Afterwards, they divorced.

[16] The pastor had "visited the building time and again during the period from 11 to 27 July 1995 and, in spite of the refusal of the plaintiff to do so, persistently demanded that the plaintiff listen to what he had to say. In addition, the pastor transported the luggage and the persons concerned to the building as requested by the husband, and possessed upon his person the duplicate key of the building at all times." (Excerpt from the judgment).

[17] As the UC was recruiting its new members among university students and subsequently married them, the abductors were mainly the parents. In the case of Jehovah's Witnesses, the failure to convert both spouses may have been a source of conflict inside married couples. Hence a high number of abductions by husbands, maybe at least 50% according to unofficial sources.

## Monitoring of the Issue

It is noteworthy that cases of kidnapping, deprivation of freedom of adult converts to new religious movements, and attempted recantation under coercion by non-state actors in Japan have been totally disregarded by human rights organizations since the first case in 1966. The US Department of State is the only institution that has monitored this issue.

Since it has started releasing its annual country report about freedom of religion or belief around the world in 1999, the issue of abduction, deprivation of freedom of adult converts to new religious movements with the purpose of religious de-conversion by non-state actors in Japan has been raised every year[18] except in 2007. Most of the victims are members of the Unification Church but Jehovah's Witnesses were also concerned. Throughout the years, both religious denominations have constantly denounced the passivity of the police and the judiciary when confronted to official complaints by victims. This situation was annually denounced and repeated like a mantra by the US reports until this year with the same sentence:

"Members of the Unification Church have alleged that police do not act in response to allegations of forced deprogramming of church members. They also claim that police do not enforce the laws against kidnapping when the victim is held by family members, asserting that Unification Church members are subjected to prolonged arbitrary detention by individuals, who

---

18According to the Unification Church, the first case of exit counseling in confinement conditions started at Ogikubo Eiko Church (Jesus Christ Church in Japan) in 1966. It was performed by Satoshi Moriyama, a pastor of an Evangelical Church, who was the driving force of the anti-UC movement.

are not charged by police." In the 2000 report it was added that "In September 1999, the Jehovah's Witnesses asserted that their members are mistreated similarly." The last known case involving a Jehovah's Witness took place in 2005.

**Further excerpts from US Department of State reports:**

*2000 Report*

> "In April 2000, a national Diet legislator raised this allegation in a committee session. National Policy Agency and Ministry of Justice officials considered the member's request for "appropriate actions," but took no action during the period covered by this report."

*2003 Report*

> "In August 2002, the courts declared "deprogramming" illegal in a case involving Jehovah's Witnesses. However, during the year, the Supreme Court rejected the Unification Church appeal in a case involving charges against family and friends of church members for kidnapping and "deprogramming." In the Unification Church's case, the court determined that the causes of the appeal were not matters involving a violation of the Constitution."

*2004 Report*

> "By its own calculation, the Unification Church claims that kidnapping and deprogramming has declined significantly in recent years. It remains concerned,

however, by the tendency of officials to judge kidnapping and deprogramming by victim's family members and deprogrammers as a family matter."

"In August 2002, the courts declared 'deprogramming' illegal in a case involving members of Jehovah's Witnesses. However, in 2003 the Supreme Court rejected the Unification Church's appeal in a case involving charges against the victim's family and the kidnappers for kidnapping and 'deprogramming.' In the Unification Church's case, the court determined that the causes of the appeal were not matters involving a violation of the Constitution. In January, the Yokohama district court ruled in favor of the defendant in a 1997 case in which two victims allege they were kidnapped and held in several apartments for nearly 5 months. The court cited a lack of evidence and peaceful conditions in captivity as reasons for the judgment. Also in January, however, the Osaka district court ruled in favor of a victim who claimed to have been abducted by her family in 2001 with the help of deprogrammers and held against her will for 2 months. Her parents and one deprogrammer were ordered to pay $2,000 (200,000 yen)."

*2005 Report*

"In 2002, the courts declared "deprogramming" illegal in a case involving members of Jehovah's Witnesses."

"A Unification Church spokesman estimated there were 20 deprogramming cases during the period covered by this report; however, at the families' request, none of the cases were reported to the police."

"According to a spokesman for Jehovah's Witnesses, members are free to practice their religion without restriction. Other than one forced confinement in January 2005, which was reported to the police after the fact, there have been no reported deprogramming cases since 2003."

## *2006 Report*

"Allegations by the Unification Church that the Government was unresponsive to claims that its members were being confined and deprogrammed decreased. Unification Church leadership reported that the number of abductions declined due to the government's increasing willingness to prosecute deprogrammers. However, church leaders continued to express concern over the government's unwillingness to prosecute abductors. According to church officials, police often refused to intercede because abductions often involved family members abducting other family members."

## *2008 Report*

"According to representatives of the Unification Church, approximately 10 to 20 practitioners were forcibly 'deprogrammed' by concerned family members during the reporting period, and in most cases, the believers "quickly gave up their faith."

## 2009 Report

"The Unification Church reports that on February 10, 2008 an adult member of the Church who had been held against his will by his family members for over 12 years was released and went to Unification Church headquarters. The Unification Church alleges no one has yet been charged and an investigation has not been conducted as of the end of the reporting period."

## 2010 Report

"The Unification Church reported five members were abducted during the reporting period. These reports could not be independently confirmed, and some nongovernmental organizations (NGOs) have accused the Unification Church of exaggerating or fabricating these reports."

"In 2008 an adult member of the Unification Church was released after reportedly being held against his will by family members and a professional deprogrammer for over 12 years. Prosecutors did not pursue the case citing insufficient evidence. The case was on appeal at the end of the reporting period."

## 2011 Report

"For several years deprogrammers working with family members have reportedly abducted Unification Church members, members of Jehovah's Witnesses, and other minority religions. The number of reported

41

cases has declined sharply since the 1990s. The Unification Church reported six members were abducted during the reporting period, two of which remained confined at year's end. One was reportedly released after police interviewed her parents. These reports could not be independently confirmed, and some nongovernmental organizations (NGOs) have accused the Unification Church of exaggerating or fabricating these reports.

In 2008 an adult member of the Unification Church was released after reportedly being held against his will by family members and a professional deprogrammer for over 12 years. Prosecutors did not pursue the case citing insufficient evidence. On October 6, a civilian panel upheld the decision not to pursue criminal charges."

## Abduction, deprivation of freedom and attempted religious de-conversion under scrutiny

Many former members of new religious movements have voluntarily left on their own and sole initiative. Other converts have changed their minds under the strong influence of various people, but without coercion. Others have experienced abduction and deprivation of freedom by their parents for the purpose of religious de-conversion and may have consequently left the movement or not. This research is focusing on people of this last category. Most of them belong(ed) to the Unification

Church[19] but a significant number of Jehovah's Witnesses[20] have also been abducted. The main reason seems to be the fact that these two "foreign" religions have practices[21] which collide with the Japanese culture. During its investigation in Japan, *Human Rights Without Frontiers* consulted various scholars but they could not provide any cases where members of other religious movements had been victims of the same practice[22].

## *(1) From parents' legitimate concerns to the abduction decision*

Parents may feel concerned when they learn that their children - even if they are educated and have reached the legal majority age – have joined a new religious movement, and quit their

---

[19]The UC claims more than 4,000 cases of abduction from 1966 to 2011 with a peak for the years 1987-1995, but only 20 or less per year since 2006. *Human Rights Without Frontiers* has however not been able to verify these figures.

[20]*Human Rights Without Frontiers* visited the Japanese branch of the Watch Tower Bible and Tract Society in Ebina City (outside Tokyo) and was given a chart with annual statistics: between 1992 and 2001, more than 150 Jehovah's Witnesses (mostly women) were abducted, deprived of their freedom and submitted to unsolicited exit counseling. This was corroborated by anti-cult journalist Kazuhiro Yonemoto.

[21] The UC does not forbid its members from participating in Buddhist or Shinto rituals on the occasion of family events such as births or funerals but the mass blessings of youths during which Reverend Moon and his wife unilaterally match young men and women for a future marriage and become their True Parents is problematic. It can indeed lead to some strong and understandable reaction of the biological parents as they may perceive it as usurpation of their natural relation with their children, a loss of their free will and a form of psychological subjection. Concerning Jehovah's Witnesses, the ban on any participation in other religious rituals (Shinto at New Year, Christian at marriages or Buddhist at funerals) and in national events creates alienation from the rest of the family and society.

[22]There are however some marginal exceptions. Kazuhiro Yonemoto mentioned one abduction case concerning a member of the Japanese Yamagishi movement.

job or interrupted their studies to devote their whole life to it. Their fears increase when they hear directly or indirectly about the negative media coverage concerning the said movement[23]. At a loss, they look for an association or individuals with whom to consult (former members of such movements, religious ministers, cult-watchers, anti-cult activists and associations). In search of a solution to their anxiety, they may finally come across exit counselors and may be invited by them to attend study sessions during which they are told how thoroughly wicked and evil the incriminated religious movement is. Their discourse instills more fear in their minds and success stories of abduction by other parents may induce them "to rescue" their loved one(s) by any means, including abduction. In this way, family members may be slowly convinced that there is no alternative solution other than abduction, isolation from other co-religionists, coercive persuasion and exit counseling leading to de-conversion and sometimes to conversion to another religion (usually Evangelical Protestantism)[24].

It is not easy to find a parent who wants to testify about the abduction of his son or his daughter. In 1995, Mrs. S.A. was

---

[23]This was particularly the case in 1992, when Hiroko Yamazaki, a famous athlete, and Junko Sakurada, a former idol singer and actress, announced they had joined the UC and participated in a UC mass wedding ceremony. This fueled many negative media reports on the UC.

[24]The exit counselors avoid frightening terms such as abduction, confinement or deprogramming and prefer "softer" and more socially acceptable words such as "rescue" from the movement, "custody", "persuasion" and "family discussion". In this way, they cannot be accused of perpetration of or incitement to illegal acts. Most exit counselors are Evangelical pastors or faithful with a background of de-conversion.

abducted for the third time[25] by her mother and father (she was then 35 years old) with the help of other members of the family. Her father, K.S., testified to *Human Rights Without Frontiers* as follows about their psychological preparation by third parties before the last attempt:

> *My wife and I were not religious people but like most Japanese, we occasionally had some Buddhist practices. We were advised to take part in meetings of the Anti-UC Parents Association held in a Christian Church in Azabu (Tokyo). Afterwards, we visited a Protestant church in Niitsu City, in Niigata Prefecture, driving for three hours each way every weekend to participate in the anti-UC study session. There were usually 50-80 parents in a situation similar to ours. The sessions comprised some Biblical training meant to help us convince our children of their errors, testimonies of parents who had managed to remove their children from the UC and instructions about the implementation of the rescue operation. Once we had decided to take action, we had private meetings with the pastor. He told us to bring the relatives and friends who would help us and gave us all sorts of strict instructions concerning the logistics. We rented an apartment from someone who had managed to remove his daughter from the UC after a successful exit counseling program.*

---

[25] She was deprived of her freedom during one week in 1983 (she pretended to recant), two months in 1993 (she escaped) and about two months in 1995 (she faked her recantation). She could not be de-converted.

Another victim who holds a PhD in environmental sciences and has a job in a well-known institute was abducted on 1 January 2011. She testified to *Human Rights Without Frontiers*:

> *"As my mother told me after the confinement, she visited the Shinjuku West Church of the UCCJ[26] and visited Kimiaki Nishida who was engaged in so-called 'mind control' research. She said she had four consultation sessions with exit counselor Takashi Miyamura. As part of an ordinary family like mine, my mother would never have thought of kidnapping and confinement."*

### *(2) Planning the abduction*

The abduction procedure must be carefully prepared. The location of the confinement premises must be carefully selected and adapted to the upcoming situation so that the confined person cannot be seen or heard and cannot communicate at all with the outside world. A rental contract must be signed and in most cases the apartments are rent by a sympathizer of the anti-UC activists or a parent who succeeded in the deprogramming to his child. Parents and relatives must be ready to serve as guardians day and night for an undetermined period, which can range from a few weeks to several months or years in exceptional cases. This may disturb their professional life or necessitate its interruption.

The usual arguments put forward to deceive the convert so that he/she voluntarily comes to the site of the planned

---

[26] UCCJ: United Church of Christ in Japan.

46

abduction are a visit to the parents, an invitation to a restaurant or a family event. As the abduction cannot be physically carried out by the sole aged parents, it usually necessitates the participation of several people, first of all close relatives[27]. These persons must be aware that they share the responsibility of the abduction and that the penal code provides for prison terms from 3 months to 7 years.

### (3) Carrying out the abduction

Under cover of anonymity, the victim abducted on the night of 1-2 January 2011 reported to *Human Rights Without Frontiers* as follows:

> *"I had come to my parents' on 1 January. We went to the local Shinto shrine as most Japanese do on the first day of the year and in the evening, my father started to argue about my new faith. Suddenly, the living-room was filled with people, including my uncle, my aunt, a biology teacher and a male nurse. They surrounded me. I grabbed my mobile telephone on the desk. As I resisted, they pushed my arms more strongly while my sister forcibly took away my telephone. I started screaming. Dressed in a nightgown, I asked for a change of clothes, to no avail. Grabbed tightly at my*

---

[27] Masashi Yoshimura who graduated from Kyoto University as civil engineer told *Human Rights Without Frontiers* that in 1987 his mother had been advised by members of an anti-UC Parents' Association to hire people from the Hokkaido Group, a mafia-like group, to perpetrate the abduction of her son and she did.

*arm, I went out through the entrance and found a black vehicle I had never seen. I was pushed inside. Ahead of our car ran a white car in which my sister and the biology teacher had taken a seat. The cars stopped in front of a three-storey apartment named 'Espoir Shirakawa'. It was around 1:30 am. I was firmly taken up the stairs to the second floor."*

Apart from this typical pattern of abduction, there were also a few cases of abduction carried out in exceptional circumstances, such as the one of Ms Hiroko Tomizawa who won her case in a civil court in 2002. She said to *Human Rights Without Frontiers*:

*"On 7 June 1997, at 2 pm, my father who is a former police officer, relatives, five private detectives, and members of an anti-Unification Church group (about 20 people in all) made a surprise attack on a Unification Church in Tottori with weapons including stun guns, iron pipes, and chains. The group destroyed the glass in the entrance door, unlocked the door, interfered with Church activities, attacked four Church members, injured them, and kidnapped me. I was pushed into a station wagon and taken away.*

*However, they didn't take me directly to Osaka. Instead they took a detour to Shikoku and kept me for three days in a room on one of the highest floors of a resort condominium in Naruto.*

*On 10 June, after 10 pm, I was handcuffed, taken out of the room and pushed again into the station wagon by force. We took the ferry to Osaka via Awaji Island.*

*On 11 June, we arrived in Osaka where I was put in confinement in the room of an apartment on the 10<sup>th</sup> floor."*

In another exceptional operation, a husband and wife were abducted at the same time by the two families. On 22 September 1996, Tsutomu Tojo and his wife Kumiko participated in a Buddhist memorial service in remembrance of a family member's death and went afterwards to another relatives' house. Kumiko told *Human Rights Without Frontiers*:

*"While resting after having tea, the door of the room suddenly opened. Surprisingly, not only my relatives but also my husband's came in. We were forced into two separate vans and taken to two different places of confinement. I did not have enough power to resist. So, I cried out my husband's name but my voice could not reach him. It was incredibly shocking."*

Masashi Yoshimura who graduated from Kyoto University as a civil engineer and also practices martial arts, shared his abduction story (1987) with *Human Rights Without Frontiers*:

*"My mother had planned my abduction with the help of yakuza of the Hokkaido Group, a Japanese mafia, because after a first attempt of persuasion without coercion she had been told I was a difficult case. I was abducted in broad daylight on the street. Four men grabbed my arms and legs, threw me into a taxi against my will, handcuffed me and took me directly to an airport in Nagoya. A Cessna was waiting for us. We were the only passengers. I was taken to Hokkaido and kept in a building of the Hokkaido Group for two months and a half. Other rooms were also*

49

*rented for two other abductees during my stay. Fortunately I managed to escape. I cannot imagine how much my parents paid for this failed operation. I filed a complaint on criminal grounds but the Prosecutor's Office dismissed it.*

### *(4) Isolation conditions*

In the Sapporo "Lost Youth Compensation Cases" against the Unification Church, the majority of the 21 plaintiffs – all defectors from the Unification Church - admitted the existence of physical restraint on their freedom of movement during the exit counseling as it is testified in their cross-examinations. Only two acknowledged they were "under house arrest" and three testified they could move freely in and out of the room.

In 2001, Kozue Terada was abducted and taken to an apartment in Osaka. She testified to *Human Rights Without Frontiers* as follows:

> *Apartment No.1005 of the Shin Osaka Heights had three bedrooms and a dining-room / kitchen. It was equipped with a futon mattress and appliances including a refrigerator and an electric oven, but there was no telephone and no television. The front door was locked and reinforced with a security chain and a custom-made chain, both padlocked. Unless the lock and chains were released, it was not possible to open the front door. All windows and glass doors were locked with special devices including security closers.*

Some abducted UC members testified that they had no or only restricted access to medical assistance during their confinement[28].

The complicity of the exit counselor in the deprivation of freedom is clearly attested to in Case No. 1732 (Lost Youth Compensation) filed with Kobe District Court in 1994, during the interaction between the UC lawyer and pastor Takazawa:

*Q: Do you sometimes arrange places for confinement?*

*T: Sometimes. Depending on the situation, I may be obliged to propose some places.*

*Q: Do you also instruct them that the rescue operation needs the cooperation of their relatives?*

*T: That is right.*

*Q: You advise them to assemble as many relatives as possible?*

*T: Well, right. (...)*

*Q: When a turn of action draws near, you discuss the date of confinement and other details with the parents concerned, don't you?*

*T: What do you mean, the date?*

*Q: I mean you need to arrange the detailed plans, say, a UC follower will come home so and so, date. So, you*

---

[28] Y.H., a pregnant woman married to a Korean citizen and living in Korea, was abducted by her parents during a visit to her family in Japan. During her 3-month confinement, she was denied proper medical assistance and lived under heavy stress, which made her very anxious about the future health of her future baby. Her own mother had been abducted by her husband several years before and quit the UC after being confined for several weeks, Y.H. was finally allowed to recover her freedom before her delivery.

*bring the relatives on the day, arrange the apartment for confinement beforehand, etc.*

*T: Such things are naturally arranged by the family concerned.*

*Q: Aren't you involved in the preparation?*

*T: That is inevitable. I have to be aware of their plan, however passively.*

In Case No 458 about a donation issue dealt with by the Maebashi District Court, Takasaki Branch (1993), pastor Yoshio Shimizu (United Church of Christ in Japan) said:

*Q: How many people have you attempted to persuade to leave the UC?*

*T: I remember the names of over 50 people.*

*Q: For the persuasion, you confine the UC followers somewhere?*

*T: You mean I carried it out?*

*Q: Do you mean you have not carried out the confinement?*

*T: What is the definition of the confinement?*

*Q: It may involve locking windows, hiding shoes or keeping constant guard, etc. (...)*

*T: There are such cases.*

*Q: Can't you persuade them without resorting to such methods?*

*T: There are cases that required them.*

Exit counselors have become more and more cautious after pastor Mamoru Takazawa was condemned on two occasions in the aforementioned civil cases filed by Kozue Terada (2004) and Hiroko Tomizawa (2002). Moreover, an increasing number of anti-cult activists disapprove of unsolicited exit counseling exerted in conditions of deprivation of freedom.

### (5) *Disappearance*

Once the convert has been abducted and deprived of his/her freedom, the person should be considered missing. However, the Japanese law enforcement actors do not view this situation as a case of disappearance when the parents or the relatives – the perpetrators of the abduction – do not declare it and moreover inform the employer and the neighbors in various plausible ways that he/she will not come back at all or only before long. The police, when alerted by a third party, consider it is a family matter. Spouses may start some research but there are very few cases where the abducted person is married and as she/he is usually transferred to a remote place, it is very difficult, if not impossible, to locate him/her.

*Human Rights Without Frontiers* met Takashi Usami, the fiancé of an abducted person, who was determined to find his loved one and showed a lot of ingenuity in attempts to do so. He attached a cell phone with GPS to the car of his fiancé's father to track his movements and find her whereabouts. That is how he managed to talk to her after almost three years. In the meantime, she had been convinced through exit counseling to leave the new religious movement.

In another case reported to *Human Rights Without Frontiers*, the fiancé hired private detectives and finally managed to locate his beloved.

### (6) **Unsolicited and forceful exit counseling by third parties reflecting a competition for followers**

53

De-conversion attempts using coercion in physical and psychological isolation conditions are mainly performed by pastors and members of Protestant churches with the assistance of former members of new religious movements

Exit counseling programs that comprise presentations of the Protestant interpretation of the Bible and focus on the alleged contradictions or errors in the doctrine of the targeted movement with regard to the Bible clearly reflect a situation of competition between two religions. While such an ideological fight might be considered legitimate on the "free market of religions" and in agreement with the principle of freedom of expression, the use of conditions of protracted confinement or restraint imposed on individuals cannot be condoned in the light of international human rights standards.

The expression "protective persuasion" used by the exit counselors can hide another reality: coercion, intimidation, and threats.

Kozue Terada told *Human Rights Without Frontiers*:

> *"On the morning of October 29th 2001, my uncles and younger sister left the apartment for work, and three people, my father and two aunts, remained to keep watch over me.*
>
> *Around 2:00 pm, Rev. Mamoru Takazawa of the Kobe Shin Church came to the apartment. I protested to Rev. Takazawa, saying, "This is a forced confinement!" Takazawa said, "Yes, this is a forced confinement", adding, "But your father and mother are confined,*

*too." Rev. Takazawa insisted that he was "requested to engage in the discussion" and stayed for about two hours criticizing the Unification Church doctrines.*

*At 2:00 pm on 30 October, Rev. Takazawa came to the room. Ignoring my desires, he continued to force me to have a dialogue with him. I said, "I don't want to be here! I am going to call the police. Let me borrow a cell phone!" As I extended my hand, Rev. Takazawa got emotional and said, "Even if a policeman comes, as soon as he finds it is about the Unification Church, he will collaborate with me, saying 'Keep on your good work!'" Rev. Takazawa took five to six name cards of policemen from his wallet, and emphasized, "I have a connection with the police."*

*Since that time, Rev. Takazawa came by almost every day until the last week of November, staying for about two hours each time, giving me the coercive exit counseling. During those sessions, he attacked my personality, calling me "retarded," "psycho," "a person like a murderer" and "one with a face like a slug in June." During the confinement, I suffered a nightmare in which I was abused by my father in confinement almost every night.*

*Around 10 November, Rev. Takazawa came to apartment No.1005 with Atsuyoshi Ojima, who was a lay assistant of the Western Japan Evangelical Lutheran Church. Ojima came by almost every day until my release, criticizing the Unification Church doctrines."*

The coercion is also obvious from the minutes of Case No. 1732 filed with Kobe District Court in 1994, in which on 21.05.1996 the UC lawyer asked Pastor Takazawa questions about an escape attempt of a confined UC member (referred to as the Okamoto incident):

> *Q: In that incident, did he jump off to the ground?*
> *T: He did not mean to jump off but he tried to escape. His family dashed to him and pulled him back but in the ensuing scuffled, he went off the balcony and fell down to the ground.*
> *Q: You mean he was heavily wounded in his escape attempt?*
> *T: That is correct.*
> *Q: His escape attempt indicates that he did not like to be forced to hear your persuasion talks.*
> *T: I guess so.*
> *Q: And he was not in a situation in which he was free to get through the entrance.*
> *T: You are right.*

It appears clearly that the exit counseling sessions were also used to proselytize under coercion. In the minutes of Case No. 1732 filed with Kobe District Court in 1994, one can read the following interaction between the UC lawyer and pastor Takazawa on 21.05.1996:

> *Q: How many members does your church have?*
> *T: About 130. About 60-70 people take part in religious services.*
> *Q: How many are there who left the UC?*
> *T: Now, roughly half of them.*

Moreover, their advisory sessions comprising Biblical training also attracted anxious parents and relatives. An obvious of abuse of psychological weakness…

Coercion was so strong in the case of Kiyomi Miyama that she had her marriage annulled to prove that her recantation was sincere[29].

### (7) Price of a "rescue operation"

Out of love, parents are ready to pay huge amounts for the sake of their children. *Human Rights Without Frontiers* has been unable to collect reliable data about the expenses engaged in abduction, confinement and exit counseling. Renting a van, renting a room or a house and remodeling it for confinement purposes for an unforeseeable period of time entails major expenses.

Moreover, *Human Rights Without Frontiers* collected testimonies suggesting that exit counselors had been paid by parents for their activities but could not verify such allegations. From one case to another, the alleged amounts varied between 4 million yen (40,000 €) and 10,000,000 yen (100,000 €)[30]. Unofficially, journalist Yonemoto was told by the police that the average price was 4 million yen. Yonemoto was also informed by an anti-UC pastor that an exit counselor without any religious motivation had proposed to a concerned mother a

---

[29] She had really lost her faith at that time and she was used by anti-UC activists in other exit counseling operations but she joined back the UC after some time.

[30] According to Kiyomi Miyama who was abducted and confined twice during 6 months and 29 months, Miyamura's average rate for rescuing 'cult members' was 40,000 €. According to Sayuri Hara, her parents regularly gave envelopes with certain amounts of money to pastors and exit counselors. She also read in her mother's notebook that her parents had borrowed around 30,000 € from an uncle.

remuneration of 10 million yen when she was considering an abduction.

The 2002 judgment by the Osaka High Court quotes an abducted female Jehovah's Witness S.S.[31] as saying about a pastor who confined her: "He is engaged in the business of coercing Jehovah's Witnesses to renounce their faith by means of confinement upon request from family members of Jehovah's Witnesses, receiving a large sum of money as a reward under the pretext of donation for the activity, in fact, acting as a so-called deprogrammer."   In the files of the Japanese branch of the Jehovah's Witnesses movement, the amount of $10,000 was mentioned by the victim.

An interesting document given to *Human Rights Without Frontiers* is a letter addressed by a grandmother to her grandchild Hideo Kawashima in 1996, in which she said she gave 4.78 million yen (47,800 €) to her daughter and son-in-law to cover the costs of his "rescue operation" (which was unsuccessful).

### (8)  Background and motivation of the exit counselors

The exit counselors are usually pastors and lay people of Evangelical and Pentecostal churches[32] who use the concerns of

---

[31] Acronym of the lady who wants to remain anonymous.

[32]According to journalist Kazuhiro Yonemoto, around 200 pastors of one specific denomination were involved in "protective persuasion" and "unsolicited or forceful exit counseling" for the purpose of de-conversion from new religious movements and conversion to Protestantism in the first twenty years of the phenomenon. For various reasons (age, possible lawsuits, negative publicity around the issue and awareness of the psychological damage caused by their persuasion techniques) their number has dramatically decreased and just a dozen might still be active now.

converts' families as an opportunity to fight against a competing heresy, and who exploit the anxieties of the parents[33] to try to evangelize them. They do not carry out abductions but they are fully involved in the preparatory phase: awareness-raising of parents through sessions and meetings with other parents who successfully carried out abductions. In some cases, abducting parents consulted them by telephone during the operation according to interviews of victims.

The most frequent names which came up during the interviews and the investigation by *Human Rights Without Frontiers* are:

Satoshi Moriyama, the pastor of Ogikubo Eiko Church (Jesus Christ Church in Japan). He was the first Christian minister to conduct forced conversion through kidnapping and confinement in 1966. He passed away in 1996;

Yasutomo Matsunaga, the pastor of the Niitsu Evangelical Church in Niigata prefecture (Japan Alliance Christ Church);

Mamoru Takazawa, the pastor of the Kobe Shin Church, an independent Evangelical church;

Takeo Funada, the pastor of Kyoto Seito Church (Jesus Christ Church in Japan);

Yoshio Shimizu, the pastor of Gyoda Church (United Church of Christ in Japan). He is a former member of the Unification Church;

---

[33]Such parents follow Biblical training sessions on the alleged ground that they will be better equipped to argue with their children on theological issues. They are also requested to attend religious services.

Masayuki Hiraoka, the minister of Japan Evangelical Lutheran Church. He died in 2009;

Tadaharu Takayama, the pastor of Kurashiki Megumi Church (Japan Alliance Christ Church);

Sakae Kurotori (female), the pastor of Totsuka Church (United Church of Christ in Japan).

Other religiously motivated exit counselors:

Tamiya Taguchi, the former director of a UC training center. Afterwards, he became a member of an Evangelical Church. He died in 2002.

Pascal Zivi, a member of the Hitsujigaoka Church (Jesus Christ Church in Japan) and founder of the Sapporo-based *Mind Control Institute*. He wrote a book called *"Escape from Mind Control"*[34].

Another exit counselor who is often mentioned is Takashi Miyamura. He is not known to have any religious affiliation. He is the director of an advertisement agency.
Psychologists are not known to be involved in exit counseling in a confinement situation.

---

[34]Pascal Zivi was born in France in 1957. He learned judo and went to Japan in 1980 to improve his abilities. There, he met an Evangelical missionary and became a Christian. In 1994, he created the "Mind Control Institute". He has no known relevant background in psychology. He claims to have made studies at an Evangelical Bible School.

*(9) "Happy endings"*

The confinement of the convert can come to an end in various ways: voluntary release by the abductors after the (supposed) de-conversion;[35] after the failure of the exit counseling; after release by external actors; and after escape by victims.

Y.K., a female Jehovah's Witness, was abducted twice by her parents near the shop where she was working. In 1998, after three days, she was released after her brother had informed her congregation. The second time (1999), she was kidnapped at 4.45 am and taken to a place that was reached after two hours' drive. After four months of confinement, she managed to escape.

In 2009, H.K. who was then 29, was abducted by her parents and was driven two hours to a remote location, where she was confined for two months and subjected to exit counseling. In the meantime, her fiancé and co-religionists looked for her, found her confinement place and visited it with a lawyer. She told *Human Rights Without Frontiers*:

> *"When the bell rang and my father opened the door, I was surprised to hear familiar voices. My fiancé, members of my church and a lawyer were standing outside the entrance door. They asked me if I was there*

---

[35]Some converts simulate the de-conversion. As most of them were not really religious before joining the new religious movement and were just nominally Buddhist, it cannot be said that after their religious destructuration they went back to their original religion. In a number of cases, the de-conversion was part of a proselytizing scheme of Evangelical churches. According to unofficial internal statistics of the UC, 60-70% of the people exposed to exit counseling in confinement conditions left the movement and only 30% kept their faith.

*against my will. I said 'yes' and I left the apartment with them. I was really happy. Afterwards, I tried to contact my parents but they did not answer my calls, my emails or my letters. It is a pity."*

A victim who wants to remain anonymous holds the record of the shortest confinement period (24 hours) and of the most acrobatic escape. She said to *Human Rights Without Frontiers*:

*"On 3 January 2011, at about 2:40 am, while my parents and my sister were sleeping, I cautiously closed the sliding door separating my room and my sister's. I took my handbag and opened the sliding window to the balcony. I was then outside on the second floor and in front of me at arm's length, there was an electricity pole. I went over the wall of the balcony, stretched my arm, held the pole's picket, moved onto the pole and climbed it down falling on my hips down to the ground. The apartment was too high for me to jump down. I might have been badly injured."*

### *(10) Follow- up of complaints by the police*

On 20 April 2000, Jin Hinokida, a member of the Japanese Diet, took part in an official hearing of the Diet to which Setsuo Tanaka, Director-General of the National Police Agency, Norikiyo Hayashi, Detective Superintendent of the National Police Agency, and Yuuki Furuta, Director-General of the Criminal Affairs Bureau of Ministry of Justice, had been summoned to answer concrete questions about their dealings with cases of abduction and confinement.

On this occasion, Jin Hinokida denounced the passivity of the police in a number of cases such as that of Hiroko Tomizawa, who was abducted in 1997[36] by a group of 20 people including her parents and relatives, confined for 15 months and subjected to unsolicited exit counseling. Tottori Police Station then failed to take due measures although it had been duly alerted. The police also waited for two years before sending the prosecution documents on six people to the Tottori District Prosecutors' Office but failed to list the names of the other assault members[37]. The Prosecutor refused to start criminal proceedings. In a subsequent civil court lawsuit, the parents and the exit counselor were declared liable and ordered to pay a small symbolic compensation.

During the same hearing of the Diet, Jin Hinokida fiercely criticized the complicity of the police in the abduction case of Mitsko Ishikawa, and was quoted as saying:

> *"Today, I will submit the evidence that the police are involved and are accepting abduction and confinement[38]. A criminal who abducted and confined a UC member had made a plan sheet. I have that original. In the sheet, it is written the date to do what, and also how to respond if the victim resists.*

---

[36] Hiroko Tomizawa, then aged 26, had been abducted a first time by her parents in June 1994 and confined for 80 days before being able to escape.

[37] Hiroko Tomizawa's father was a retired policeman and could probably rely on the complicity of other policemen.

[38] HRWF footnote:In Japanese culture, parents tend to consider their children as their possession. According to journalist Kazuhiro Yonemoto, the necessity of a Child Abuse Prevention Law was not discussed until around 1995. The concept of child's rights and domestic violence is also a recently imported value, though not necessarily recognized and accepted by society, like the concept of human rights in general. Hence the attitude of the police who consider abduction of adult children as a "family matter."

*Moreover, the father of Mitsko Ishikawa contacted the Akishima police station on 14 May 1998 before carrying out the plan, made the plan "authorized" and then carried it out."*

However, when the Japanese wife of a Korean citizen was abducted and all the interventions to move the police proved to be unsuccessful, Jin Hinokida called the Korean Embassy. As a result, the concerned Yamagata Prefecture Police rushed to the place of confinement and released the victim of the abduction and confinement.

On 14 May 2010, Tsukasa Akimoto (Liberal Democratic Party), Member of the Upper House and the Audit Committee, heard a number of government representatives on the role of their institutions in cases of abduction and deprivation of freedom with the purpose of religious de-conversion. Victims of abduction and confinement have not often filed complaints because the police often takes sides with the abducting parents as it was obvious in the case of Miss A.S. who told *Human Rights Without Frontiers* under cover of anonymity: "After I had escaped, I called the police and I told them my family had confined me because they opposed my marriage. After talking to my father, they started reprimanding me and criticizing me. Finally, they handed me over again to my parents and I was confined again by them until I escaped again!"

### *(11) Follow- up by the judiciary system*

Not many complaints have been filed by victims of abduction and confinement, because of reluctance to bring legal actions against parents but also because from the experience of other abductees they do not trust the management of such incidents by the judiciary. Moreover, the policy of the judiciary when faced with religiously motivated cases of abduction and confinement has failed to deliver justice.

> **All known complaints filed jointly against abducting parents and exit counselors have been declared ineligible for criminal proceedings by prosecutors[39]. Only some complaints before civil courts have been taken in consideration.**

- *Toru Goto* who was victim of abduction and confinement for 12 years was released in 2008. In June 2008, he filed criminal charges against those involved in his confinement. On 9 December 2009, the Prosecutor's Office decided to waive indictment on the ground of insufficient evidence.

- *Emiko Motoki* was abducted and confined from 13 to 25 November 2002. She was released by the police. She submitted a criminal complaint on 1 December 2002 but the Prosecutor's Office dismissed the case on 5 July 2004.

---

[39] *Human Rights Without Frontiers* knows 24 cases for which there were criminal complaints between 1980 and 2008. In 1980, Miss Mitsue Tashiro, Miss Tomoko Okubo and Mr. Hideo Mima filed a complaint against the mental hospital where they were confined, and an exit counselor named Tomigoro Goto. In all the other cases, criminal complaints were filed against the perpetrators of abduction and confinement but some of them did not do it against their parents. The most recent cases are Miss Hiroko Tomizawa (2000), Mrs. Kozue Terada (2002), Mrs. Emiko Motoki (2002) and Mr. Toru Goto (2008) who were interviewed for the purpose of this report.

- *Kozue Terada* was abducted and confined from 28 October to 27 December 2001. She submitted a criminal complaint to the police in Osaka on 19 February 2002 but on 15 September, 2004, Osaka Prosecutor's Office dismissed the case on the grounds that it did not deserve a criminal proceeding.

- *Hiroko Tomizawa* was abducted and confined from 7 June 1997 to 30 August 1998. She submitted a criminal complaint to the police in Tottori on 25 April 2000 but on 6 August 2000, the Tottori Prosecutor's Office dismissed the case.

- *Rie Imari* was abducted and confined for the second time on 10 January 1997. She was coming out of a restaurant with her husband when eight people (her parents and relatives) jumped on them and pushed her into a car. She was subsequently deprived of her freedom for 5 months. She was released on the assumption that she had given up her faith. As soon as she was free, she filed a complaint for a criminal case. Yokohama District Prosecutor's Office waited until 26 March 2002 before deciding that the case did not deserve a criminal proceeding. In the meantime, Rie Imari and her husband (he had been injured during the abduction) seized a civil court with another complaint against her parents and the two pastors involved in unsolicited exit counseling at her confinement place (6 January 1999). They were claiming a financial compensation of 15 million yen (150,000 EUR) for various damages (loss of salary, injuries, etc.) and the injunction to stop another attempt. On 23 January 2004, Yokohama District Court dismissed the case. On appeal, Tokyo High Court upheld the decision on 31 August 2004. They then seized the Supreme Court which suggested a friendly settlement. The only claim that was kept in the settlement was the promise to respect each other's religious freedom.

When *Namiko Katagiri* was abducted and confined by her parents during 170 days in 2001-2002, her husband tried to lodge a complaint with the police but they refused to file it as they considered it was a family matter. Therefore, he started a civil court procedure against his parents-in-law. On 3 September 2002, there was a legal settlement, which stated that the parents deeply apologized, promised not to repeat such an action and to pay the amount of 2 million yen to their daughter and their son-in-law.

### (12) Psychological consequences for the abducted converts: Post-traumatic stress disorder

Some abducted converts experienced post-traumatic stress disorder (PTSD) and others not.

In 2004, Keiko Ikemoto[40] and Masakazu Nakamura[41] published a study entitled "Forced deprogramming from a religion and mental health: A case report of PTSD" in the International Journal of Law and Psychiatry[42]. The unnamed

---

[40]Clinical Research Institute, National Minami Hanamaki Hospital, 500 Suwa, Hanamaki, Iwate 025-0033, Japan.
[41]Counseling Service Association, Nishitokyo, Japan.
[42] Issue 27(2004), pp 147-155. Full article available online at http://sciencedirect.com

and religiously unidentified victim[43] was a Jehovah's Witness, according to information obtained by *Human Rights Without Frontiers*. The victim was a 32-year old female without any personal or family psychiatric past history. She was kidnapped and kept in solitary confinement by her family for 20 days. According to what the researchers wrote about the posttraumatic disorder she experienced, after she returned to her house, the psychiatrist diagnosed a moderate to severe depressive state. As she was afraid to stay alone, she stayed at her friend's house for three weeks. She was too fearful to ride on a bicycle; noises made her irritable; when somebody talked in a rhythm similar to that of the clergyman, she could not bear it; she complained of anxiety and insomnia; she experienced the sensation that of being bound hand and foot at night. The victim also had guilt for recanting her faith and could not restore her relations with her parents.

*Conscience problems[44]*

> "Although she once renounced her faith, it was intolerable to realize when she calmed down that it was herself that was being deceived. She blamed herself for having betrayed her fellow adherents at the time of her release from confinement."

*Damage to her relations with her parents*

> "When the therapist asked her about the relationship with her parents, she said: 'I wished to be dutiful to my parents (...). They broke my heart. It was

---

[43]The patient wanted her privacy to be respected.
[44]Quotation from the study « Forced deprogramming from a religion and mental health: A case report of PTSD ».

shocking that my family should be disinterested in my confinement. I can forget what others did but I can't forget what my family did to me. I want to have my name struck out from my family register,' she said in a rather indifferent manner. Nevertheless, her anger was expressed in her speech and facial expression."

"After one year, the therapist met the patient. The patient said: 'I'm doing well at work, but I feel slightly listless since that event. I can't forgive my parents even now. My feelings towards my parents are similar to those for a rapist. I feel strained whenever I recall that event.' For her parents' part, as they had noticed the serious influence of the confinement and betrayal on her, they wanted to apologize to her. However, she would ever wish to meet her parents again."

In their conclusions about the relation between exit counseling under coercion and PTSD, Keiko Ikemoto and Masakazu Nakamura referred to James R. Lewis, a scholar in religious studies, and David G. Bromley, a professor of sociology[45]:

"Lewis and Bromley (1987) reported that among 36 of those who had experienced involuntary counseling, 61% showed a floating and altered state, 47% nightmares and 58% amnesia, and that the incidence of these symptoms was lower among those

[45]HRWF footnote: For information see "The Cult Withdrawal Syndrome: A Case of Misattribution of Cause?" by James R. Lewis and David G. Bromley, Journal for the Scientific Study of Religion, Vol. 26, No. 4 (Dec., 1987), pp. 508-522, (article consists of 15 pages). http://www.jstor.org/pss/1387101

who had voluntary counseling (41%, $n$=29), although it was still higher than voluntary seceders, who did not require other's participations (8-11%, $n$=89). Their results showed that even voluntary counseling is harmful in the context of mental health. This might indicate that the situation in which autonomy in religious belief is harmed can cause trauma and PTSD. In the present case, another cause of trauma was the moral sense of the patient, which was injured by her transient withdrawal from her faith, resulting from involuntary counseling."

Abducted converts are not the only victims of PTSD. Another clinical psychologist[46] told *Human Rights Without Frontiers* that abducting parents also experienced PTSD whether their operation had been successful or not. Both abducted and abductors would need followup counseling, some said.

***

The PTSD phenomenon was also investigated by the journalist Kazuhiro Yonemoto who interviewed three victims. In his book, 'Our Disturbing Neighbors - a woman's saga after her rescue from the Unification Church' he reported about three women who had left the Unification Church after being kidnapped and detained by their parents with the purpose to have them recant their faith. The women. had all been members of the Unification Church in the past; they had been "kidnapped suddenly one day by their parents, and confined in apartments" while they were church members; they had been

---

[46]Prof. Katsuya Tsukukoshi was teaching clinical psychology as a lecturer at Komazawa Women's University for ten years before dealing with PTSD victims in private consultations.

persuaded to recant their faith during their confinement; and had all finally resigned from the UC.

In the summer of 2002, Yonemoto met Asako Shukuya (44) and wrote about her:

> *"It had already been six years since she had left the Unification Church. Asako was in an over-stimulated state for the better part of the day. Her 'head was spinning at high speed and wouldn't stop,' which was known as "hyperphrenia of the brain" in psychiatric medicine. In addition to atopy and over-stimulation, she had symptoms of depression, nightmares, sleeping disorder, and she complained, 'Each day is so difficult.'*
>
> *She saw her parents once in a while, but when the meeting with them became warm and embracing, somehow she ended up vomiting later. It would be understandable if she felt nausea when the atmosphere was grim and threatening, but it was just the opposite."*

Reporting about Asako's doctor (then employed by Medaka Clinic of Yokohama City), he quoted him as saying: *"In the case of Asako-san, her PTSD is a severe and complex case caused by long-term experiences of trauma (shock that injures the mind) that is sustained and repeats itself, rather than a simple, one-time incident."*

S.N., a victim interviewed by *Human Rights Without Frontiers*, declared under cover of anonymity[47], that since 1993 he has been suffering from post-traumatic stress disorder.

> *"Sometimes I was depressed and I could not sleep. I could not concentrate any more. I cannot understand that parents can do that to their children. They did not want to meet my future wife and they do not want to see their two grandchildren. I am ready to reconcile but first, I want them to say they regret what they did to me. It is still an open wound almost twenty years later."*

### *(13) Consequences for the family relations*

It must be kept in mind that it is out of love that parents abduct and confine their children, which can lead to paradoxical situations and unexpected results.

When Hiroko Tomizawa was kidnapped for the first time in 1994, she protested her confinement by deciding to die through fasting but her father was empathetic to the extent he went on hunger strike with her[48].

While the planned objective of the parents is to save their adult children from a perceived danger, the outcome of their strategy is usually a painful rupture. Some parents have lost much of

---

[47]S.N. is from a Catholic family. He was educated in Catholic school institutions. His aunt was a nun. His exit counselor was a Lutheran pastor that had been recommended to his parents by the Catholic Church they were attending.

[48] See footnote nr 35.

their money, their time, their health and their children when the latter have freely chosen not to give up their new faith.

There are cases of restoration of the family relations (the quality and the frequency of contacts vary) but there are also situations where children keep away from their family out of rancor or fear of a new abduction. Some parents regret their choice, while others do not feel any remorse. *"We try to forgive but it is difficult and it is only through our faith that we can make some progress"*, some converts say.

Parents and children are both victims of the alleged and well-publicized "solution" proposed by the exit counselors: painful rupture of family relations, defiance on both sides, negative consequences on their physical and psychological health, frustration, loss of jobs and income, an unforeseeable outcome on both side, etc.

In the Case No. 1732 filed with Kobe District Court in 1994, the UC lawyer asked pastor Takazawa:

> *Q: Do you advise the parents that, as their children dedicate their lives for their faith, they must also devote their lives to rescue them?*
> *T: Surely, I tell them so.*
> *Q: Do you also advise them to make up their minds, even giving up their jobs, in order to rescue their children?*
> *T: Unfortunately, there occur such cases from time to time.*
> *Q: Rather than 'from time to time', if the deprogramming needs months of efforts, the parents are constantly pressured to quit their jobs, aren't they?*

*T: Because parents generally judge that their children's life is more precious than their jobs, they naturally come to the inevitable conclusion themselves. This is the reality.*

A mother, Tomiko Kimura, told journalist Kazuhiro Yonemoto that she appreciated her son's withdrawal from the UC but she regretted the method she had used.

Under cover of anonymity, a victim who holds a Ph D in environmental sciences and has a job in a well-known institute testified to *Human Rights Without Frontiers*:

> *"A few days after my escape, I met my father. His appearance was drastically different from what he was at the confinement room. He looked dreadful but empty-minded and distrustful, with sunken cheeks and sluggish beard. He barely walked with his back leaning forward and hands trembling, like a demented old man. With tears in my eyes, I grabbed his hands but had some arguments with him. Mother separated us apart. Obviously, my family also sustained psychological and physical damages. After all, the whole family has become the victim of a malicious crime of abduction and confinement which destroyed it while it was supposed to restore it. My confinement was short but its effects will be long"*

Y.K., a Jehovah's Witness, told *Human Rights Without Frontiers*:*"I feel sad for my parents. They have lost their contact with me and my two brothers who share the same faith. I would like to see them but I am still afraid of a possible*

74

*abduction. We were all victims of that pastor who had promised*
*to solve their problem."*

Due to the difficulties of restoring the relations parents-children, it might be useful to ask for the assistance of a neutral mediator, some suggested.

However, there were also cases where the abducted young man or woman gave up his/her faith in the new religious movement. Afterwards, some of them had a happy life without any specific religion but regretted the method employed by their parents. *"Those who had recanted their faith were expected to become Christian by their exit counselors but I did not become a Christian,"* said Koyomi to *Human Rights Without Frontiers*.

# TORU GOTO: 12 LOST YEARS

Toru Goto was born in 1963 into a wealthy family that was not religious but shared some social Buddhist and Shinto practices. While nobody could then have predicted that 12 years of his life would one day be a nightmare, perhaps the high social position and the prosperous financial situation of his father was one of the reasons for the exceptional duration of his personal tragedy. He was indeed the manager of a paper factory and had thousands of employees. He was an authoritarian figure who was used to giving orders and to be obeyed without any discussion. Toru respected him, but they were not close to one another.

### De-conversion process against Takashi, Masako and Toru

At the age of 23, Toru was studying in the Construction Department of the Science and Engineering Faculty of Nippon University when he came in contact with the Unification Church through his brother Takashi. Their younger sister Masako also joined the church later. In spring of 1987, his brother suddenly disappeared. When he re-appeared, he was totally transformed. He had become Protestant and was crusading against the Unification Church. What had happened? His parents had had deep concerns about the new orientation of their three children and wanted to take them out of the UC. They had contacted an organization of parents of former UC members called Mizukukikai, which was managed by Takashi Miyamura, the director of an advertisement agency and a non-religiously motivated exit counselor. These parents had in the past experienced the same concerns as Toru Goto's father and

77

mother. They had then abducted their adult children, confined them and successfully put them in the hands of UC-opponents to re-educate them, a process considered successful, and one that attracted the parents of other young peole who had joined the UC.

In autumn of 1987, when Goto was 24, his father asked him to meet him in a hotel room in Tokyo. Much to Toru's surprise, his mother and his brother were also waiting for him. They entered into a sharp discussion. Toru tried to go out but the door was fixed with a special device that made any escape impossible. Infuriated by the situation, he struggled with his brother and parents, who eventually overpowered him. He was confined for a week in this hotel room and every day, Takashi Miyamura brought in several former UC members to try to convince him to give up his new faith. He was then transferred to an apartment in Ogikubo, Suginami Ward (Tokyo). Convinced that there was no way out, he pretended to recant his new religious beliefs and waited for his release, in vain. In the latter days of November, he managed to escape.

Fearing another confinement attempt, Toru resigned from the Taisei Corporation, where he worked, changed his name and moved to another location. He decided to fully devote himself to church activities.

About one year later, his younger sister Masako also gave up her new religious orientation.

In 1990, Toru Goto began to communicate again with his family and occasionally visited his parents' home. They promised him that they would not try to abduct him again.

In August 1992, Toru Goto participated in the 30,000 couples' International Blessing Marriage Ceremony held in Seoul (South Korea), with his fiancée Miss Yukiko Soga.   But later her parents made her leave the UC.

Around 1995, his brother married Yoko Hoshino, a former UC member de-converted by Miyamura and Pastor Yasutomo Matsunaga of the Niitsu Evangelical Church (Japan Alliance Christ Church).

In August 1995, Toru Goto attended the 360,000 couples' International Marriage Blessing Ceremony with Kazuko Saito, his new fiancée.

### Second attempt of de-conversion of Toru Goto

On the evening of 11 September 1995, eight years after the first abduction, Toru Goto was forcibly taken into a van by his parents, his brother and an unknown man on the occasion of a visit to his family in Nishi-Tokyo City. The alleged purpose of the visit was a "family discussion" about his religious affiliation. After two hours of talk, he did not recover his freedom of movement and he was then transferred to a room in Niigata prefecture (Unit 607 at Palace Mansion Tamon) where he lived from 12 September 1995 until 22 June 1997. His place of confinement was tightly sealed, he said. All the windows and the entrance door were locked from within. He did not have any key that would have allowed him to leave the place. His parents, his sister and his brother's wife were constantly present and were pressuring him to renounce his faith. Pastor Matsunaga also visited him several times to persuade him to leave the UC.

Toward the end of December 1995, he submitted a written renunciation of faith but his parents and the pastor did not trust him and continued his confinement. In March 1996, Toru's father was hospitalized and never went back to Unit 607 at Palace Mansion Tamon. During all that time, his mother took care of her dying husband in Tokyo and Toru just stayed with his sister-in-law. His father passed away from cancer at the age of sixty-five on 22 June 1997. Toru was moved to his house in Nishi-Tokyo City to see his mortal remains; he was 'accompanied' by eight people and did not see any chance to escape. Right after the death of his father, he was transferred to an apartment in Tokyo (Ogikubo Pureisu, Room # 605). He did not have any key and he was confined there for six months.

Around the end of December 1997, he was taken to Room 804 of Ogikubo Flower Home, where he was confined for about 10 years[49].

His fiancée searched him and waited for him for 3 years, but eventually gave up hope of his return.

**Takashi Miyamura's attempts to de-convert him**

Between early January 1998 and September of the same year, Takashi Miyamura brought former UC members to room No. 804 and pressed him to leave the church. His record indicates Miyamura visited him as many as seventy-three times until September 1998. Miyamura said, "It is not I but your family

---

[49] Kiyomi Miyama was abducted and confined twice during 6 months and 29 months. She now lives in South Korea. She told *Human Rights Without Frontiers* in Seoul that Miyamura forced her to visit Toru Goto in 1998 to convince him to leave the church after she had recanted her faith and before joining again the Unification Church.

that is confining you. If you want to go out, tell your family members!" Such a reaction shows that the exit counselor was fully aware of his deprivation of freedom. His brother and his sister were also threatening: "If you don't change, you shall remain this way for the rest of your life!"

> Kiyomi Miyama, once a member of an exit counseling team, testified to *Human Rights Without Frontiers* about the situation of Toru Goto: "In 1998, I once visited Room 804 in the same Flower Home Apartment where I was confined before. Mr. Toru Goto was detained in this room. When a former member tapped on his front door, Mr. Goto's family member opened the heavy lock and let us in. One of his family members locked the door again behind us. Mr. Goto's head was drooped the whole time Miyamura was showering him with words of criticism. When we left the room, Mr. Goto's family member unlocked the front door for us and relocked it after we stepped out. I met Mr. Goto just once. I don't remember exactly how long but I think it was about 20 to 30 minutes. When I was taken to that room, Miyamura and others were already there, speaking to him. When I entered the room, Miyamura began to talk about me. He introduced me, saying, 'She is your junior alumni. (We had attended the same university). In the beginning, she did not open her mouth for six months but now she is with us.'

Mr. Goto kept looking down. I felt terrible stress in the anguished, tense atmosphere of the persuasion. I felt very, very sorry for Mr. Goto, who cast his eyes down. Therefore, I could not say anything to him. I also did not want to say anything to help Miyamura's persuasion.

While I was in the room, Mr. Goto did not move at all, he just kept looking down. I believe their aim was that because Mr. Goto showed no sign of responding to the persuasion, they brought me in hoping he might show some pride as a senior alumni of the same university; also I think they wanted to disturb him by telling him 'here's someone who resisted more vehemently than you (Mr. Goto), and in the end, even she listened to us, and left the UC."

With the passing of time, Toru Goto became so desperate that he could not help attempting to escape even by dashing toward the entrance, only to be contained by the family. He used to shout at them, saying, "Call the police!" or "I shall sue you through a lawyer!" Then the family rolled him in a futon (Japanese-style bedding) and forcibly closed his mouth. Sometimes, he was unable to breathe and almost suffocated at some points. Several escape attempts ended in failure and tighter surveillance.

From 2004 to 2006, he made three hunger strikes, two of which for 21 days and one for 30 days. His family called that "religious fasting."

**Free again after 12 years and 5 months**

Around November 2007, it looked like the family members had started arguing about whether to go on with the confinement due to the financial burdens it imposed. Renting an apartment in Tokyo easily costs 1500 – 2000 EUR.

On 10 February 2008, at around 4:00 PM, his brother, his sister-in-law, his mother and his sister suddenly ordered him to leave the apartment. He was then physically extremely weak. Dressed in his lounge wear, he was thrown down on the concrete corridor in front of the entrance door without any belongings or ID document.

On his way to the UC Headquarters, he tried to borrow some money at a police station, but to no avail as he could not reasonably explain his situation. Fortunately, he came across a UC member, who offered some money, with which he could take a taxi to reach the Church headquarters.

That evening, he was diagnosed with malnutrition and admitted to a hospital. For a while, he could barely stand on his feet.

"I can never pardon their actions. They deprived me of my fundamental human dignity as well as the most precious period of my life. Yet, my family members and Miyamura, have not yet shown any remorse or offered an apology. Miyamura even tried to divert blame from himself by saying that he never knew that the entrance door of the Ogikubo Flower Home was padlocked."

**The legal fight**

In April 2008, Toru Goto submitted a written statement to the Head of the Sugamo Police.

In June 2008, he filed a criminal charge against those involved in his confinement.

On 9 December 2009, the prosecution decided to waive the indictment of a criminal complaint on the grounds of insufficient evidence.

On 23 June 2010, Toru Goto appealed to the Tokyo Committee for the Inquest of Prosecution[50], with the hope of reopening the criminal case.

On 6 October 2010, Goto's appeal was rejected by the Tokyo Committee for the Inquest of Prosecution on the ground that there were too many doubts to judge the case as an attempt of compulsion, capture, confinement and injury.

According to the Summary of the Decision by the Tokyo No. 4 Committee for the Inquest of Prosecution, "three friends of Takashi joined to help prevent the Unification Church's possible attempt to retake the petitioner back to their hands but it was not to help prevent the petitioner to escape from the scene."

Such a statement indicates that the Committee understood that Toru Goto's family considered him a mere object, did not recognize his right to have religious beliefs of his own, and were moving him from one place to another without his consent under the alleged pretext of protecting him against the UC and avoiding his being kidnapped by the UC, as if he had no personal will, and treated him as a mentally insane person. However, Toru Goto never said he wanted to be protected against the UC. When he was freed from the illegal confinement, he rushed to the UC for assistance. He is now an

---

[50] The Committee for the Inquest of Prosecution meets in closed session and the names of the members are not disclosed. In Toru Goto's case, the Committee consisted of 11 ordinary citizens selected by lot among voters living in Tokyo. This system is similar to the Grand Jury system in the US. In order to re-open a case, it should be decided as "appropriate for prosecution" by a qualified majority of more than eight members out of eleven. The Summary of the Decision by the Tokyo No 4 Committee for the Inquest of Prosecution is written like a court decision.

active UC member who testifies on the international level against abduction and confinement and forceful de-conversion.

On 31 January 2011, he filed a civil lawsuit against his family members and the exit counselors.

Toru Goto has established the *Japanese Victims' Association Against Religious Kidnapping, Confinement & Forced Conversion*[51]. Under his leadership, the Association has approached anti-cult actors to open a dialogue with them and make them aware of the damage they have caused.

### A tentative cultural explanation of parents-children relationships in Toru Goto's case

A psychologist, Junichi Ishizaki[52], explained to *Human Rights Without Frontiers* some characteristics of the cultural background of parent-child relationships in Japan in order better to understand the family abduction-confinement phenomenon:

"Toru Goto's parents themselves might not have been particularly bad people in the eyes of the police and the Prosecutor's Office. Rather, it can be assumed that his parents and siblings who are 'good parents and children' came to harbor intense anger and hatred against him because he did not conform to their 'good' family relationship and acted as a disobedient troublemaker.

---

[51] The association was created on 8 January 2010 and has about 500 members. It aims 1) to eradicate the phenomenon of kidnapping, confinement and deprogramming; 2) to prosecute the perpetrators of these actions; 3) to take care of the victims; to raise awareness on this issue in Japan and abroad. See their website in Japanese and in English: http://kidnapping.jp

[52] Junichi Ishizaki is a professor of Kobe Gakuin University, Clinical Psychologist, PhD.

Nevertheless, why did Toru Goto's parents go to extremes to make their adult child conform to their wishes by confining him? The unique characteristics of families in Japan have probably something to do with this. There is an underlying cause that each member of family is not granted an adequate (psychological) status as an independent personality in familial relationships.

In other words, a family in Japan has a coherent interdependent unity as a whole, but the level of psychological independence of each family member is low. If one of the family members increases his level of independence in terms of his unique internal value such as his thought or faith, that threatens the psychological identity of the rest of the family members. They are not used to functioning as a coherent family while allowing independence of each family member. That binding power derived from the 'sense of unity' is strong especially because it is an unconscious one.

The culture that does not recognize the independent personality and fundamental human rights of each person fiercely rejects an emerging individual who is different from the rest and tries to make him/her conform to the will of the whole even at the expense of his/her individual internal freedom. It is a culture of "ostracism" that can be called totalitarianism. In such a family, parents who are in the position of guardians who should protect their children's human rights can turn into unreasonable rulers who violate their adult children's human rights. Furthermore, just like child-abusing parents deny the fact of their abuses by claiming 'this is discipline,' parents might not be fully aware of the meaning of their acts and consider them as 'family matters' and 'family discussions'

# ABDUCTION AND DEPRIVATION OF FREEDOM FOR THE PURPOSE OF FORCED RELIGIOUS DE-CONVERSION UNDER INTERNATIONAL LAW

By Patricia Duval, Attorney, Paris (France)

## I. The International Legal Framework

When Japan joined the United Nations (UN) in 1956, it did so with great enthusiasm and broad public support, for the international organization was seen to embody the pacified country's hopes for a peaceful world order. By joining this inter-governmental body, it agreed to abide by the UN's international human rights commitments and standards, in particular the principles articulated in the Universal Declaration of Human Rights (Declaration), adopted by UN General Assembly Resolution 217A on 10 December 1948.

The Declaration expressed its purpose very clearly:

> Whereas disregard and contempt for human rights have resulted in barbarous acts which have outraged the conscience of mankind, and the advent of **a world in which human beings shall enjoy freedom of speech and belief** and freedom from fear and want has been proclaimed as the highest aspiration of the common people,

Article 18 of the Declaration states:

Everyone has the right to freedom of thought, conscience and religion; this right includes freedom to change his religion or belief, and freedom, either alone or in community with others and in public or private, to manifest his religion or belief in teaching, practice, worship and observance.

However, the Declaration is not a binding legal treaty. In order to make human rights an instrument effectively shaping the lives of individuals and nations worldwide, more than just a political proclamation was needed. Hence, the substance of the Declaration had to be translated into the concrete and practical legal form of a binding international treaty.

On 16 December 1966, the General Assembly adopted the International Covenant on Civil and Political Rights (ICCPR or the Covenant) by which its signatories became legally bound to protect the international human rights guaranteed in these instruments. The General Assembly also adopted the International Covenant on Economic, Social and Cultural Rights on the same day. Along with the Declaration, these documents are known as the International Bill of Rights. These treaties were signed and ratified by Japan on 21 June 1979.

In Article 2.1 of the Covenant, the State Parties undertake to respect and to ensure to all individuals within their territory and subject to their jurisdiction the rights recognized in the Covenant, without distinction of any kind, such as religion amongst others.

Article 18.1 of the Covenant guarantees the right to freedom of conscience and religion in the following terms:

Everyone shall have the right to freedom of thought, conscience and religion. This right shall include freedom to have or to adopt a religion or belief of his choice, and freedom, either individually or in community with others and in public or private, to manifest his religion or belief in worship, observance, practice and teaching.

But more significant to the issue here is Article 18.2 providing:

**No one shall be subject to coercion which would impair his freedom to have or to adopt a religion or belief of his choice.**

Under these provisions, Japanese citizens are free to adopt a religion or belief of their choice and the Japanese authorities are bound to ensure that no Japanese citizen is subject to coercion that would impair this freedom. This obligation applies even in cases where this coercion is exerted by private parties independent from the State.

In particular, under Article 18.3, the State shall ensure:

(a) that any person whose rights or freedoms as herein recognized are violated shall have an effective remedy, notwithstanding that the violation has been committed by persons acting in an official capacity;

(b) that any person claiming such a remedy shall have his right thereto determined by competent judicial, administrative or legislative authorities, or by any other competent authority provided for by the legal system of the State, and to develop the possibilities of judicial remedy;

89

(c) that the competent authorities shall enforce such remedies when granted.

Therefore, the Japanese authorities are bound to enforce the prohibition of coercion exerted for example by private parties to force followers of religious denominations to recant their faith. They are also bound to make sure that appropriate remedies are granted in such cases.

In order to ensure the implementation of the Covenant's provisions, a Human Rights Committee was set up under Article 28 of the Covenant, composed of experts in the field of human rights from the State parties. The Human Rights Committee is the principal actor at the international level mandated to enforce the rights enunciated in the ICCPR.

By formulating "general comments", the Committee has opened up a new window of activity. Through such "general comments", it explains the scope and meaning of the provisions of the ICCPR and clarifies general issues as they arise in the process of implementation.

Its General Comment 22 explains the scope and meaning of the right to freedom of conscience and religion guaranteed by the Covenant. It makes it very clear that new or minority religious or belief movements are to be protected on an equal basis as traditional religions.

> 2. Article 18 protects theistic, non-theistic and atheistic beliefs, as well as the right not to profess any religion or belief. The terms "belief" and "religion" are to be broadly construed. Article 18 is not limited in its application to traditional religions or to religions and

beliefs with institutional characteristics or practices analogous to those of traditional religions. The Committee therefore views with concern any tendency to discriminate against any religion or belief for any reason, including the fact that they are newly established, or represent religious minorities that may be the subject of hostility on the part of a predominant religious community.

Therefore if hostility is manifested by members of a traditional religious community, such as a Protestant pastor involved in fighting against religious or belief minorities as in the present issue, the Japanese authorities have a duty to enforce Article 18 of the ICCPR and to make sure that the rights of the followers of such minority religion or belief are respected.

In its General Comment 22 the Committee explained further:

> 5. The Committee observes that the freedom to "have or to adopt" a religion or belief necessarily entails the freedom to choose a religion or belief, including the right to replace one's current religion or belief with another or to adopt atheistic views, as well as the right to retain one's religion or belief. **Article 18.2 bars coercion that would impair the right to have or adopt a religion or belief, including the use of threat of physical force** or penal sanctions to compel believers or non-believers to adhere to their religious beliefs and congregations, **to recant their religion or belief or to convert**.

Thus the rights protected by the Covenant are very clear: Article 18 **protects the right to retain one's religion or belief** and the Japanese authorities have to enforce this right – even if such beliefs are seen with hostility or concern by a predominant religious community or by parents of adult followers.

Any coercion on followers of new or minority religious or belief groups to have them recant their faith or convert to traditional religions, like the use of physical detention and forced "deprogramming", is illegal under the Covenant.

To ensure enforcement of the Covenant, a Protocol (the First Optional Protocol) was adopted to enable the Human Rights Committee to receive and consider, once domestic remedies were exhausted, communications from individuals claiming to be victims of violations of any of the rights set forth in the Covenant. This Protocol was optional and Japan has not yet signed and ratified it.

However, another United Nations human rights body, the Human Rights Council, an inter-governmental body within the UN system made up of 47 States responsible for strengthening the promotion and protection of human rights around the globe, was created by the UN General Assembly on 15 March 2006 (to replace the previous Human Rights Commission) with the main purpose of addressing situations of human rights violations and make recommendations on them.

In 2007, the Council instituted a new Universal Periodic Review (UPR) mechanism to assess the human rights situations in all 192 UN Member States. Under this mechanism, all UN Member States are reviewed every four years - with 48 States reviewed each year.

The documents on which the reviews are based are: 1) information provided by the State under review, which can take the form of a "national report"; 2) information contained in the reports of independent human rights experts and groups -

mandated by the Human Rights Council to address either specific country situations or thematic issues in all parts of the world-, human rights treaty bodies, and other UN entities; and 3) information from other stakeholders including non-governmental organizations and national human rights institutions.

Therefore NGOs can and should submit information to the Human Rights Council on religious freedom violations in Japan for these issues to be taken up during the UPR on Japan, the next one being in 2012.[53]

The Council also established a new Complaint Procedure – opened to individuals - to address "consistent patterns of gross and reliably attested violations of all human rights and all fundamental freedoms occurring in any part of the world and under any circumstances".

However, the Council – like its predecessor the Commission – is an inter-governmental body and is more likely to take political decisions regarding "gross and reliably attested violations of human rights", like the one adopted recently regarding Syria. On the other hand the Human Rights Committee is a committee of experts and its opinions have shown to be more independent.

During the first UPR on Japan in May 2008, violations of religious freedom have not been raised. But the Council

---

[53] For the procedure to follow and the dates: http://www.ohchr.org/en/hrbodies/upr/pages/NgosNhris.aspx

formulated the following as its first recommendation which Japan accepted for follow-up:

> Japan will consider concluding the human rights treaties listed as follows:
> - the First Optional Protocol to the International Covenant on Civil and Political Rights

In its mid-term progress report in March 2011, Japan indicated:

> With regard to the individual communications procedure stipulated in the First Optional Protocol to the International Covenant on Civil and Political Rights (...) the Government of Japan established a Division for Implementation of Human Rights Treaties in the Ministry of Foreign Affairs in April 2010, thereby giving serious consideration as to whether or not to accept the procedure. Specifically, consideration is given to such aspects as whether there are any problems in relation to Japan's justice system and legislative policy, and a system to be established for the implementation of the individual communications procedure when Japan accepts the procedure.

Thereby Japan is under pressure from the UN to adopt the Optional Protocol, which will allow individual complaints to be acted upon by the Human Rights Committee once domestic remedies are exhausted.

In the meantime, Japanese Courts are bound to apply the provisions of the ICCPR when ruling on cases of abduction and forced de-conversion of followers of religious minorities, and Japanese citizens should continue to fight in Court to have their rights enforced.

Although the same obstacles as in Japan were opposed – in particular the argument of the legitimacy of parents' concerns - positive precedent has been obtained in similar cases in other countries bound by international human rights treaties.

## II. Relevant Case Law

Abduction and forced de-conversion first appeared in the United States where many cases of so-called "deprogramming" occurred during the 1970s and 1980s.

Like what is happening in Japan these days, US Judges were reluctant at first to sanction such acts, in particular because parents were the initiators, calling for the intervention of "deprogrammers", based on what were purportedly "legitimate" concerns.

### A) United States

The few following cases show the progression of legal reasoning in dealing with these cases. Ultimately, the Courts concluded that abduction for forcible de-conversion could not be squared with the protected right to religious freedom and constituted a violation of criminal laws.

### *The Susan Peterson Case*

In 1976, a 21-year old girl involved with a religious organization called *The Way Ministry*, Susan Peterson, was held against her will by her parents and two deprogrammers. After one week, one of the deprogrammers told her that papers had been drafted to commit her to a State Institution if she refused to cooperate with the deprogramming.

After two weeks she managed to escape and filed a civil lawsuit. On 17 February 1978, a ruling was rendered in favor of Susan sentencing the deprogrammers to $ 6,000 and $ 4,000 damages respectively.

On appeal the Minnesota Supreme Court held that "when parents, or their agents, acting under the conviction that the judgmental capacity of the adult child is impaired, seek to extricate that child from what they reasonably believe to be `a religious or pseudo-religious' cult, and the child at some juncture assents to the activities in question, limitations upon the child's mobility do not constitute meaningful deprivation of personal liberty sufficient to support a judgment for false imprisonment."

This case became the key decision relied upon by the anti-cult movement throughout the United States as justification for their deprogramming activities. But the jurisprudence of Minnesota State court decision was subsequently overturned by a decision of the Minnesota Federal court in the William Eilers case.

### The William Eilers Case

On 16 August 1982, William Eilers, twenty-four, and his pregnant wife, Sandy, twenty-two, were abducted as they were leaving the clinic following Sandy's prenatal examination, on the accusation that they were involved with a cult, *The Disciples of the Lord Jesus Christ*. The team of deprogrammers had been assembled from various parts of the United States, including Texas, California, Pennsylvania, Iowa, and Ohio and flown to Minnesota at the parents' request and expense.

A civil suit was filed against the deprogrammers by Eilers during which the defendants claimed they had acted only "to exercise their constitutional rights of free speech." The deprogrammers also asserted they had no liability for what they had done because under the decision in Peterson they were relieved of any liability as agents of the parents. To them, Peterson seemed to provide safe haven for their illicit operations in Minnesota.

At the conclusion of the Eilers trial, United States District Judge Harry MacLaughlin entered a directed verdict in the plaintiff's favor on Eilers' false imprisonment count against each of the defendants. In his opinion, Judge MacLaughlin stated:

> There is also no question that the plaintiff was actually confined. Relying on the Minnesota Supreme Court's decision in *Peterson v. Sorlien*, 299 N.W.2d 123, 129 (Minn. 1980), the defendants contend that there was no actual confinement because there is evidence that the plaintiff consented to the defendants' actions. At least by the fourth day of his confinement the plaintiff, in contrast, has testified that he merely pretended to consent in order to gain an opportunity to escape. The plaintiff's apparent consent is not a defense to false imprisonment. Many people would feign consent under similar circumstances, whether out of fear of their captors or as a means of making an escape... Under the circumstances, the court finds, in agreement with many other authorities, that plaintiff's

97

apparent consent is not a defense to false imprisonment. [Citations omitted.] The court therefore holds, as a matter of law, that the plaintiff has proven the necessary elements of false imprisonment.

After suggesting several alternatives available to the defendants, if in fact there were a need for psychological assistance, Judge MacLaughlin stated:

At no time did the defendants attempt, or even consider attempting any of these alternatives during the five and one-half days they held the plaintiff, the first five of which were business days. Instead they took the plaintiff to a secluded location with boarded-up windows, held him incommunicado and proceeded to inflict their own crude method of "therapy" upon him -- methods which even the defendants' own expert witness had condemned. Well aware that the police were searching for the plaintiff, the defendants deliberately concealed the plaintiff's location from the police.

Judge MacLaughlin's opinion in the Eilers case thus nullified the defense of the Peterson case. William Eilers was awarded $10,000 in damages, but in addition the family members and others settled out of court for $50,000.

### The Thomas Ward Case

On November 24, 1975, Thomas Ward came to visit his family in Virginia for the Thanksgiving holiday but he was kidnapped at the airport and taken against his will to a location where deprogrammers restrained, assaulted, and deprived Ward of sleep.

The United States District Court "concluded that since the parents of the plaintiff were motivated to act by their concern for the well-being of their son, the requisite discriminatory class bias was absent." However, the United States Court of Appeals for the Fourth Circuit overturned this ruling by finding (*Ward v. Connor*, 654 F.2d 45 (4th Cir. 1981):

> While we do not quarrel with the court's assumption in regard to such parental concern, the complaint sufficiently charges that the defendants were motivated to act as they did not only because they found the plaintiff's religious beliefs intolerable, but also because of their animosity towards the members of the Unification Church. This, in our opinion, stated a discriminatory motive sufficient to support a claim under the statute.

### The Britta Adolfsson Case

In *People of the State of Colorado v. Dennis Whelan and Robert Brandyberry*, two professional deprogrammers hired by Britta Adolfsson's Swedish parents, successfully argued before the trial court that they were not guilty of a criminal conspiracy and kidnapping under a "choice of evils defenses." This defense was based on the defendants' claim that the victim had been "brainwashed" by the religious group of which she was a member and not therefore exercising "free will" with respect to her religious beliefs.

The National Council of Churches filed a friend of the court brief where they noted that the necessity defense raised was the same defense used in the Eilers case in Minnesota. The brief pointed out that the Eilers court specifically held that the defendants' failure to attempt to use the lawful alternative available to them effectively eliminated the "choice of evils" necessity defense citing Eilers, 582 F. Supp. at 1099.

The Colorado Court of Appeals adopted the argument made by the National Council of Churches in its amicus brief, deciding to preclude the use of the "choice of evils" defense. (*People of the State of Colorado v. Robert Brandyberry and Dennis Whelan*, No. 88-1741, slip op. at 11 (Colo. Ct. App. Nov. 23, 1990)).

### The Jason Scott Case

By a judgment of 3 October 1995, the United States District Court for the Western District of Washington found the plaintiff Jason Scott's abduction by a team of three deprogrammers had violated Scott's civil rights. The jury awarded Scott $ 875,000 in compensatory damages and $4 million in punitive damages, 3$ million against the three deprogrammers and $1 million against the anti-cult organization, Cult Awareness Network ("CAN").

The leading deprogrammer and CAN filed motions to the Court for a new trial and for reduction in damages. The Court denied the motions with the following reasoning:

> Mr. Ross objects to the amount of both the compensatory and punitive damages awarded. Mr. Ross claims that the evidence was insufficient to support the amount of compensatory damages, the

100

amount of punitive damages was unreasonable, and the jury's award was motivated out of passion.

Considering the extensive testimony on the destruction of Mr. Scott's family life as well as his physical and emotional problems after the deprogramming, the Court finds that evidence does not justify a new trial or a reduction of compensatory damages. Again, numerous witnesses verified the extent of these injuries. (...)

As to punitive damages, Mr. Ross also argues that the award was excessive. Specifically, Mr. Ross asserts that the damages bear no relation to the harm suffered or to the amount necessary to deter his future conduct. The Court disagrees. The Court concludes not only that there is a sufficient relationship between the harm and Mr. Ross' conduct, but that the remaining reasonableness factors also weigh heavily towards upholding the jury's punitive damages award. As noted above, the evidence supported the large award of compensatory damages. Moreover, Mr. Ross' use of terminology cannot avoid the uncontradicted evidence that he actively participated in the plan to abduct Mr. Scott, restrain him with handcuffs and duct tape, and hold him involuntarily while demeaning his religious beliefs.

A large award of punitive damages is also necessary under the recidivism and mitigation aspects of the factors cited in Haslip. Specifically, the Court notes that Mr. Ross himself testified that he had acted similarly in the past and would continue to conduct "deprogrammings" in the future. Further, Mr. Ross faces no future criminal or civil liability for his conduct.

Finally, the Court notes each of the defendants' seeming incapability of appreciating the maliciousness of their conduct towards Mr. Scott. Rather, throughout the entire course of this litigation they have attempted to portray themselves as victims of Mr. Scott's counsel's alleged agenda. Thus, the large award given by the jury against both CAN and Mr. Ross seems reasonably necessary to enforce the jury's determination on the oppressiveness of the defendants' actions and deter similar conduct in the future.

Accordingly, the Court finds that both the compensatory and punitive damages awards were reasonable and well founded in the evidence.

The judgment was later appealed but the Appeals Court confirmed the findings of the District Court. The intention of the judges to fight recidivism was fulfilled as subsequently CAN filed for bankruptcy and was dissolved.

## B) Europe

In Europe similar sentences have been pronounced by the Courts and parents have not been excluded from criminal proceedings. We will just cite a few examples here.

In **Germany**, a sentence to a prison term of three and five months on probation for false imprisonment and bodily harm sanctioned the attempt of two British deprogrammers to persuade a 32-year old member of the Church of Scientology, Barbara S., to resign from this community in the village of Herrsching. To that end the two British sequestrated the 32-year old in a holiday home and "treated" her, after she was asked by her mother under false pretenses to come from Munich to Herrsching.

The two deprogrammers claimed to have acted on the initiative of the mother. But the statements of the two in an attempt to blame the mother alone were not followed by the Court.

In its judgment of 29 December 1987, the District Court Weilheim in Upper Bavaria found the accused guilty of "a jointly committed false imprisonment legally coinciding with a jointly committed bodily harm" and convicted them to three and five months suspended jail terms.

The mother was prosecuted separately subsequently and in her case the prosecution was discontinued on the basis of her paying a penal fine of 2.000 DM at the time - by reason of her confused mental state.

In **Switzerland**, in March 1989, Sandro P., who had joined the Hare Krishna movement, was kidnapped by four men on the initiative of his parents who were both members of SADK, a Swiss anti-sect association. Their purpose was to submit him to a deprogramming treatment. The leading deprogrammer, an English citizen, later got a 6-month suspended prison sentence and the two parents got 10-month suspended prison sentence.

Recently, in **France**, in August 2011, a couple forced their 24-year old daughter into their car in Nice, handcuffed her and drugged her, to take her in a wheelchair to Corsica. The parents claimed to have been advised to do so by an anti-sect association to take her away from her boyfriend's influence, who was allegedly Antoinist.

Both parents were subsequently charged in September for kidnapping and sequestration.

The European Court of Human Rights, which enforces the European Convention on Human Rights and Fundamental Freedoms that 47 countries have signed and ratified and which contains strikingly similar freedom of religion or conscience provisions to the ICCPR, has ruled that the State cannot participate or endorse such abductions for forced de-conversions by private parties.

In its decision *Riera Blume and others v. Spain* of 14 October 1999, the Human Rights Court found a violation of the Convention by the Spanish State even though the abduction and "deprogramming" had been performed by the parents and an anti-sect association, *Pro Juventud*:

> 29. (…) From the undisputed account of the facts it appears that, in accordance with the judge's instructions, the applicants were transferred by Catalan police officers in official vehicles to a hotel about thirty kilometers away from Barcelona. There they were handed over to their families and taken to individual rooms under the supervision of people recruited for that purpose, one of whom remained permanently in each room, and they were not allowed to leave their rooms for the first three days. The windows of their rooms were firmly closed with wooden planks and the panes of glass had been taken out. While at the hotel the applicants were allegedly subjected to a "deprogramming" process by a psychologist and a psychiatrist at *Pro Juventud*'s request. (…)

35. In the light of the foregoing, the Court considers that the national authorities at all times acquiesced in the applicants' loss of liberty. While it is true that it was the applicants' families and the *Pro Juventud* association that bore the direct and immediate responsibility for the supervision of the applicants during their ten days' loss of liberty, it is equally true that without the active cooperation of the Catalan authorities the deprivation of liberty could not have taken place. As the ultimate responsibility for the matters complained of thus lay with the authorities in question, the Court concludes that there has been a violation of Article 5 § 1 of the Convention.

The European Court of Human Rights has also ruled that the right to religious freedom has to be protected no matter the hostility expressed by relatives towards one's religious choices.

In its landmark decision of 10 June 2010 *Jehovah's Witnesses of Moscow v. Russia*, the Court has reasserted the right to conduct one's life in a manner of one's own choosing and in particular the right of self-dedication to religious matters.

The Court found that:

111. It further appears from the testimonies by witnesses that what was taken by the Russian courts to constitute "coercion into destroying the family" was the frustration that non-Witness family members experienced as a consequence of disagreements over the manner in which their Witness relatives decided to organise their lives in accordance with the religious precepts, and their increasing isolation resulting from having been left outside the life of the community to which their Witness relatives adhered. It is a known fact that a religious way of life requires from its

followers both abidance by religious rules and self-dedication to religious work that can take up a significant portion of the believer's time and sometimes assume such extreme forms as monasticism, which is common to many Christian denominations and, to a lesser extent, also to Buddhism and Hinduism. **Nevertheless, as long as self-dedication to religious matters is the product of the believer's independent and free decision and however unhappy his or her family members may be about that decision**, the ensuing estrangement cannot be taken to mean that the religion caused the break-up in the family. Quite often, the opposite is true: **it is the resistance and unwillingness of non-religious family members to accept and to respect their religious relative's freedom to manifest and practise his or her religion that is the source of conflict**. It is true that friction often exists in marriages where the spouses belong to different religious denominations or one of the spouses is a non-believer. However, this situation is common to all mixed-belief marriages and Jehovah's Witnesses are no exception. [emphasis added]

Concerning the argument of "brainwashing" made by the Russian authorities to justify the banning of Jehovah's Witnesses' activities, the Court found this concept legally inexistent and totally inapplicable to consenting followers:

128. The Russian courts also held that the applicant community breached the right of citizens to freedom of conscience by subjecting them to psychological pressure, "mind control" techniques and totalitarian discipline.

129. Leaving aside the fact that there is no generally accepted and scientific definition of what constitutes "mind control" and that no definition of that term was

106

given in the domestic judgments, the Court finds it remarkable that the courts did not cite the name of a single individual whose right to freedom of conscience had allegedly been violated by means of those techniques. Nor is it apparent that the prosecution experts had interviewed anyone who had been coerced in that way into joining the community. On the contrary, the individual applicants and other members of the applicant community testified before the court that they had made a voluntary and conscious choice of their religion and, having accepted the faith of Jehovah's Witnesses, followed its doctrines of their own free will.

The same should apply to followers of new religious movements in Japan, who have freely adhered to their community. No argument of family "concerns" or labelling of conversion as "brainwashing" can justify abduction and forced de-conversion attempts.

These practices constitute violations of the right to freedom of religion or conscience and kidnapping, illegal under international human rights law and national criminal law.

# CONCLUSIONS

# RECOMMENDATIONS

*Human Rights Without Frontiers* has collected data coming from various objective and reliable sources that confirm the long-standing and persistent, though declining, existence of the kidnappings for the purpose of forced conversion: a well-known investigation journalist[54], a former member of the Diet, abducted converts to a new religious movement, abducting parents, lawyers, psychologists and scholars in religious studies. Court decisions against parents and an exit counselor also confirm the issue.

The phenomenon has massively affected the Unification Church and to a lesser extent Jehovah's Witnesses. The Unification Church was targeted right from the beginning of its mission in Japan. The reasons were multi-fold but some of them were decisive: 1) the new religious movement was coming from Korea, a country arousing hostility in society for historical reasons; 2) it was claiming to be Christian and was perceived as a dangerous heresy by Protestant Churches; 3) the movement had controversial practices colliding with the Japanese family culture such as the usurpation of the parents' consent in the choice of the fiancé(e) and the mass marriages celebrated in South Korea or in the US by Reverend Moon and his wife,

---

[54]*Human Rights Without Frontiers* tried to contact English-speaking leaders of anti-cult movements in order to get their perspective but never got any reply despite reminders.

claiming to become the new True Parents of the converts; 4) a number of negative court decisions concerning the so-called 'spiritual sales'[55] and the 'lost youth compensation' were largely covered by the media; 5) their methods of recruitment of new members; 6) their fundraising practices.

Additionally, a general mistrust towards religions and a pervasive climate of social hostility toward new foreign religious movements[56] did not play an insignificant role in the persistence of the issue.

Interreligious competition also contributed to the phenomenon and the fight against a 'heretical' group was at least tolerated if not encouraged behind the scenes by the leaders of their denominations. .

Cultural habits can explain individual and social attitudes but cannot justify them, certainly not in light of international human rights law. The abduction, the confinement or deprivation of freedom of movement, the so-called 'family discussions' or 'protective custody' imposed on adults, and unsolicited or forceful exit counseling of converts to new or other religious movements for the purpose of religious de-conversion in Japan must be unambiguously condemned as incompatible with human rights principles and eradicated; freedom of thought and of conscience, freedom of religion or belief and freedom of movement are grossly violated by non-state actors with the passive complicity of the police and in total impunity. With

---

[55] These so-called "Spiritual sales" are a practice where UC members sold to the public so-called Hanko (sealed stamps) ,a rosary or other items, to allegedly free people from the fateful destiny of their ancestors, sometimes referred to as indulgences with promises.

[56] The gas attempt of Aum Shinrikyo and the controversial activities of the Soka Gakkai contributed to the creation of such a climate.

citizens denied protection against such crimes, they are thus treated in differentially and unfairly, based on their religion. The issue is also thus one of religious discrimination.

Japan's government should thus make more efforts to integrate the international human rights culture and law in society and legal institutions, and revise practices of its law enforcement forces and its judiciary that are inconsistent with Japan's international legal human rights obligations.

### *Human Rights Without Frontiers* recommendations

### To Japanese Authorities

- The appointment of an Ombudsman for Religious Freedom in the Ministry of Justice with the power to investigate violations of religious freedom due to abduction and deprivation of freedom with the purpose of forcing people to change their religion.

- The Japanese Diet (Parliament) should hold public hearings involving victims, police authorities and judicial authorities, as well as international experts and international human rights lawyers familiar with legal standards on deprogramming developed by the ECHR, US and European Courts.

- The National Police Agency (警察庁 *Keisatsu-chō*) should conduct an independent internal review of how the cases documented in this report have been handled, and follow-up with investigations of these crimes as well as the failure to initiate such investigations in the past.

111

- The Police and Judicial authorities should inform the public of the law and clear guidelines regarding steps that may and may not be taken by families regarding religious practices of their children.

- The Police and Judicial authorities should prosecute the persons directly and indirectly involved in the abduction of adults for the purpose of making them change their religion under coercion and in confinement conditions, and should not refrain from initiating criminal cases.

- Any officials found to have neglected their responsibilities or to have colluded with the perpetrators of crimes should be punished accordingly.

- Official apologies should be offered to victims.

- Japan should sign and ratify the First Optional Protocol to the ICCPR.

**To Japanese and International Civil Society**

- Japanese citizens should defend their fellow citizens against kidnappings, by reporting violations of the law to authorities and protesting if authorities do nothing.

- Journalists should conduct investigations of cases of the coercion of family members to bring greater exposure, transparency, public awareness and dialogue. Mass media should objectively document and expose the problem.

- Local and international human rights organizations should address these issues, to encourage more victims to come forward and provide greater exposure and accountability necessary to reform. Japanese human rights NGOs and international NGOs should thus assist the Japanese government to abide by its human rights obligations.

- Local and international NGOs should make reports on the issue for submission to the United Nations Universal Periodic Review process and to the UN special rapporteur on freedom of religion, and to the UN Human Rights Committee prior to review's of Japan's compliance with the International Covenant on Civil and Political Rights (ICCPR).

**To the International Community**

- Japan's bilateral partners should express concern about Japan's failure to protect citizens from crimes. In particular, the United States Department of State and the European Union should focus on these problems in exchanges with Japanese authorities and in reports. The US Commission on International Religious Freedom should devote appropriate attention to this issue.

- Members of the United Nations should raise the issue in reviews of Japan's human rights record in the course of the Universal Periodic Review The UN Human Rights Committee should focus on this problem during its next periodic review of Japan's compliance with the Covenant.

113

- The UN Special Rapporteur on Freedom of Religion or Belief should visit Japan to investigate the kidnapping with impunity of members of religious groups, and report on the issue to the Human Rights Council.

www.ingramcontent.com/pod-product-compliance
Lightning Source LLC
Chambersburg PA
CBHW072325290526

45794CB00002B/746